Why Trade Contractors Fail and How to Prevent It©

A Handbook of Financial, Operational, and Marketing Procedures to Help Trade Contractors Succeed©

By

Dr. James (Jim) McCain
The Business Doctor

Thirty Years Helping Small Businesses Survive and Prosper

ISBN: 978-1-84961-113-8

Published by: RealTime Publishing

Limerick, Ireland

TABLE OF CONTENTS

No, or inadequate/incomplete, marketing and sales plan

Can't get bonded

Bidding jobs too low

Supervisors not handling the job well

Change orders not implemented

Projects falling behind schedule

Lawsuits

Backlog increasing

Lead times unrealistic

Disputes between contractor manager, company owner, and customers

Poor communications from field to company management

APPENDIX

NOTE TO READERS

On the following pages you are going to read many practical, hands-on methods and procedures for improving every aspect of the trade contractor's business operations. In several instances you will see company names such as ABC, Inc. or ABC Contracting. These are fictional companies designed to show you how the procedures described in this book work in a trade contractor's business. Please keep in mind that these are *representative* methods and procedures for the *typical* trade contractor. But since the size and scope of trade contractors' operations vary immensely, you will need to tailor the solutions shown for your specific company. If you have any questions about applying these methods and procedures, please do not hesitate to contact me via my email address (mccain97@aol.com) or through my website (bizdrsolution.com).

Thanks and best of luck,
Jim McCain

PART ONE

DO I RUN THIS BUSINESS OR DOES IT RUN ME?

A fair question that trade contractors need to ask themselves is "Do I run this business or does it run me?" Unfortunately, too many times the business runs them.

It runs them because, while most trade contractors understand the technical aspects of their crafts inside out, many know little about the business side of their companies: marketing, project scheduling, cost control, handling customer demands, cash flow, collections, banking relationships . . . and the innumerable other business methods and techniques that spell the difference between success and failure of a trade contractor's enterprise.

According to BizMiner, of the 823,830 building (non-single-family), heavy/highway, and specialty trade contractors in business in 2000, 28.4percenthad failed by 2002. Every year, thousands of trade contractors, whether in business for two years or 20 years, face bankruptcy and business failure, leaving behind unfinished private and public construction projects.i

With the economy stalled and prices for parts and materials increasing, the importance of handling the business side of trade contracting assumes even greater significance. Shrinking profit margins put a strain on small businesses struggling just to stay alive. Under these dire circumstances, understanding how to control costs and stay on schedule producing high quality products and services is paramount.

That's where I come in. For the 30 years I've spent helping small businesses regain or strengthen profitability, I have come to recognize one pervasive truth: trade contractors don't focus on business fundamentals because they're too involved with the technical nuts and bolts of their professions. They are so busy working *in* their business that they have no time to work *on* their business.

Trade contractors recognize problems, but many don't understand how or why the problems happened or how to fix them. Some run out of cash, some fall behind project schedules, some don't realize they have too many or too few workers before they run out of money or miss scheduled completion dates, some don't know how to account for expenditures. I could go on and on; the list of business-related problems is virtually endless.

Not that trade contractors are unique when it comes to business problems; they certainly aren't. Even the largest commercial companies exhibit the same problems mentioned here. The difference is that the larger companies have the luxury of hiring specialists to fix business problems. Smaller businesses, most of them operating on shoestring budgets such as trade contractors, can't afford to employ full-time specialists in finance, accounting, inventory control, scheduling, quality, productivity, cost control, and the many other specialties that often spell the difference between success and failure of a commercial enterprise.

And quite often, forces beyond their control compound their problems. For example, a faltering economy, union demands, inflation, and parts and material shortages. All of these play a role and tend to exasperate the trade contractor's struggle to keep his head above water.

While the bookstores are crammed full of business advice for small businesses such as trade contractors, more often than not theoreticians write them; they're the worst possible advisors because they have no direct experience in working as trade contractors or servicing them. Trade contractors get impatient with such books that teach theory and those that contain endless lists of so-called sophisticated business methods and techniques that take a Philadelphia lawyer to interpret. Learning from such books is not their bag (nor mine). *But a book that shows trade contractors how to repair deficient parts of their business, spoken in the language they understand, gets their attention.* And that's the secret of my method and the focus of this book. I show trade contractors how to address problems and strengthen their companies and never throw academic lessons at them or inundate them with business theory. Indeed, Part One of this book describes the most common business problems vexing trade contractors (See *Warning Signs That Your Trade Contracting Business Is in Trouble*). Then, Parts Two through Parts Six reveal workable solutions in plain-spoken language.

For a list of the types of trade contractors and subcontractors I'm referring to see the appendix of this book.

Who Am I (The Business Doctor), and What Makes Me an Expert In Helping Trade Contractors?

The following ad from my website says it all:

> "Are your business problems more complex? Do they require a deep background in functional business problem-solving? BUSINESS WORKS CEO Dr. Jim McCain, a 30-year veteran with over 450 satisfied business clients, provides general business consulting. Contact the Business Doctor today for a free two-hour business physical. "

I help companies solve business problems. **I specialize in**

working with small businesses, especially trade contractors (building, electrical, HVAC, plumbing, among others). A few of my accomplishments include:

- ❖ Saved a carpentry and cabinet contractor $146,000 in its first year operating costs by reducing waste in man hours, inventory, and vehicle maintenance.
- ❖ Increased revenue for an electrical contractor $80,000 by implementing an employee incentive program.
- ❖ Prevented corporate bankruptcy for a $1.5 million laser saw company by applying financial controls and accurate job costing procedures.
- ❖ Assisted a $10 million per year emergency power service provider with the implementation of sales reporting, labor burden calculations, job descriptions, incentive plans, and human resource procedures. The company later grew to just over $100 million in sales volume.

My website *Business Works* (http://www.bizdrsolution.com/) has proven to be an invaluable aid to small business owners and managers. From there, clients such as trade contractors have downloaded literally thousands of business manuals, employee manuals, business plan templates, employee evaluation forms, and a host of other important business documents tailored to their individual businesses.

For 15 years, during my early career, I was a professor at the State University of New York (SUNY). During that time I wrote for many business publications and was a frequently sought-after speaker at local, national, and international meetings.

To learn more about the large number of services I provide my clients see the appendix of this book or visit http://www.bizdrsolution.com/ .

Warning Signs That Your Trade Contracting Business Is in Trouble

Any number of signs can point to impending trouble. The successful trade contractor juggles many balls in the air, and dare heii let one slip through his fingers, it could well have a cascading effect and cause him to drop other balls. For example, if the trade contractor allows his customers to miss or lag in scheduled payments, that squeezes cash needed to pay for supplies, thereby forcing vendors to cut off the supply of parts and materials. The entire trade contracting operation comes to a screeching halt.

In another example, the project falls behind schedule and customers insist on penalty payments, (or more likely take them out of future payments or delay them until they are satisfied), and eventually stop making payments. This also has a cascading effect as employees quit because of short or missed paychecks and the project shuts down or lags until the contractor can find additional funds and hire and train new employees.

Unfortunately, there are too many more of other likely scenarios that end the same way: the business either shuts down or continues operating for a short period of time until the lack of cash or profits triggers the inevitable bankruptcy.

Let's examine the major potential trouble spots:

- ❖ Poor or inexpert financial systems
  - o Inadequate financial planning
  - o You have financial planning problems if:

    - You haven't spoken to your banker in a week.

    - You don't know how much money is in your business account.

    - You don't have last month's P&L report on your desk within 10 days of the end of last month.

    - You have *any* accounts that are past due.

    - Your sales are lower or flat, compared to last year.

    - You only see your accountants when they are filing your quarterly tax returns. (Ninety percent of accountants limit their participation to tax filing; a sparse 10 percent are actually involved in management control accounting.)

  - o Cash flow is tight, projections inaccurate. Cash to a trade contractor is equivalent to blood to a human being. Without blood, the body dies; without cash to pay bills and wages, the business folds. Realistic and timely cash projections allow company owners and managers to arrange enough cash on hand to meet the demands of the business. Without advance planning, cash shortages may very well threaten the life of the business *even when sales are booming.*

o Receivables turning slowly and building. Other than initial outlays of borrowed or invested money, the business derives its need for cash by collecting customer receivables. Slow customer payments, especially those long over thirty days, may cause the business to go hat in hand to the bank and borrow enough money to keep the business afloat until customers pay their bills (assuming the bank will extend additional credit; it most likely will not in today's economy). And loans are prohibitively expensive. Too many loans and before you know it interest on the borrowed principle eats up profits and forces a loan default.

   ▪ Customers stretching average receivables from 30 to 45, 60, even 90+ days. Orders could be increasing while cash flow is decreasing—a major symptom of this recession hitting home. Contractors get squeezed between late payers and tighter credit terms, putting even healthy companies at risk.

o Vendors demand cash on delivery. This is a sure sign that the business may headed in the direction of the bankruptcy court. Vendors hate to cut off customers' supplies but they have no choice when trade contactors don't pay their bills. No parts and materials, no completed projects. No completed projects, no payment from customers. This vicious cycle renews itself with vigor.

o Lines of credit at their limit; banks won't renew. Lines don't even have to be at their limits for banks not to renew. Banks typically extend credit lines on the strength of receivables, inventory, and personal asset guarantees.

o Past due bills piling up. Another sign that the business is headed in the wrong direction. And another danger point that may signify the end of the trail. It points to the need for cash flow planning for starters and prompt collection of customer payments or renegotiating terms with suppliers.

o Profits trending down. This is usually the first indication that the financial health of the business is headed south. If, over a period of time (two quarters in a row), profits continue declining, something is wrong with the business and the reasons need to be determined before a crisis occurs.

o Lines of credit at their limit; banks won't renew or extend further credit, and that could well signal the demise of the business without a fresh infusion of capital from investors or owners.

❖ Inadequate accounting controls

o Job estimates are unreliable. There is nothing as fundamental to the business of trade contractors as estimating costs and profits accurately. Low estimates lead to a sudden and unexpected demand for cash when the project is underway, and that creates a cash crisis, never an easy problem to solve in a business that operates on thin margins. Higher than needed estimates require additional borrowing costs and this saps profits because the trade contractor must pay interest on loans that are not producing income.

o Bidding jobs too low. This is a worst-of-the-worst situation. It reduces both profits and cash flow and can lead to a quick insolvency.

o Can't get bonded. The kiss of death in an industry where bonding is often a prerequisite for operating the business.

❖ Project management that fails to manage

o Supervisors not handling the job well. Sometimes these individuals are relatives, which make matters far more complex. Management incompetence creates all kinds of headaches: loss of project control, dissatisfied employees, ordering of excess parts and materials, falling behind schedule, poor quality, and cutting corners because of rushed jobs, excessive overtime . . . . Well, you get the point. Investing in and training competent managers and supervisors is a basic requirement for a successful trade contracting business.

o Change orders not implemented. Every trade contracting business needs an orderly procedure to handle revisions to drawings and specifications. Not to have such a procedure invites trouble. Contractors implement change orders to increase profits, improve safety or quality, or reduce costs. Failure to implement such change orders may cause customer complaints, cost overruns, and even catastrophic failures. *Change orders are not to be trifled with.* Unfortunately, employees in the field do not always pay close attention to change orders because management doesn't insist they do.

o Projects falling behind schedule. The most visible part of falling behind schedule is antagonized customers. They may demand penalty payments, possibly ask for their money back, maybe file a complaint with the state consumer affairs office or Better Business Bureau. Worst case, they may sue (see *Lawsuits*). One thing for sure: they will *definitely* not give the trade contractor additional business. They'll probably bad mouth the trade contractor, and once that happens, the word spreads fast. Of course, there's also the not inconsiderable matter of lost income when project schedules go awry.

o Lawsuits. There is no sense in belaboring this point. Most trade contractors cannot afford the luxury (read expense, damaged reputation, and lost business) that comes with lawsuits. A trade contractor operating on the financial edge may tip over once somebody files a lawsuit.

o Backlog increasing. There's a difference between a backlog increasing due to incoming orders or slipped schedules. Both have unintended consequences. If the backlog increases too much, too fast it's possible that due date promises made to customers will slip, thereby causing customer complaints and invoking penalties. If the existing schedule slips, those same penalties may kick-in, and by so doing so, they'll drive up the cost of the project and lower its profit margins. Yet another example of the cascading effect of multiplying problems.

- o Lead times unrealistic. Finishing projects ahead of schedule and under budget is acceptable, even admirable. However, if this happens too often it's an indication that something is amiss in the planning cycle—meaning the company may be shortchanging itself for additional orders. Lagging schedules, on the other hand, are *always* unacceptable and lead to all the problems described in the paragraphs above. Both conditions indicate the need for further analysis to improve lead time forecasts.

❖ Communication problems

- o Disputes between contractor manager, company owner, and customers. Confusion reigns. This is an indication that all parties to the transaction have not clearly defined their duties and responsibilities, or have not kept up with the events that threaten them (for example flood, fire, or blizzard).

- o Poor communications from field to company management. Management has not schooled worksite supervisors to submit field reports or report exceptions (slipped schedules, missing or defective parts and materials from vendors, employee discontent, equipment failures, and so on). Perhaps the field superintendent is inexperienced, or perhaps he is the wrong person for the job. The name of the game is "no surprises." Surprises indicate that operations are not under control.

PART TWO

GETTING YOUR FINANCIAL HOUSE IN ORDER

We'll start with financial matters because cash and profits are the lifeblood of any business, especially small businesses such as trade contractors. An unexpected drop in cash or profits can spell the difference between company life and death. If a trade contractor doesn't have his financial affairs in order and if he doesn't understand how receivables, lines of credit, collections, and similar critical financial issues affect his company, he won't be in business for long.

This section covers the following topics:

Financial planning
Cash flow
Estimating
Breakeven analysis
Budgeting and forecasting
Profit and expense control
Account receivables and collections
What you need to know about accounting

In this section (Part Two) and each of the following five sections (Parts Three, Four, Five, and Six), I will identify matters that demand the attention of company owners and managers, and I will explain how to handle those matters with practical, time-tested methods and procedures. No theory, just get-the-job-done techniques that work.

For most of the procedures shown in this section the company owner and his accountant will put their heads together to determine which of those procedures best suit the business at this stage of its development.

FINANCIAL PLANNING

My experience over the past thirty years of helping small companies, including trade contractors, succeed and flourish has been that most small businesses do not go under because they lack technical savvy; rather, they lack capital and don't understand how to handle cash. They don't plan to fail, they just fail to plan. "Mike, the plumber" has no difficulty when he is only responsible for managing himself, his truck, his tools, and his cash. The problem arises when he takes on apprentices or a couple of other plumbers who then expect Mike to manage their trucks, tools, and cash needs. The need for space, overhead, inventory, customer relations, reports, accountability, job definition, and the like suddenly become things that Mike had never factored into the equation.

Accounting and financial planning issues tend to be unpopular among entrepreneurs. This is somewhat strange, since money is so important to most entrepreneurs that they are obsessed with it. They struggle to raise it, save it, borrow it, and spend it wisely. Some find the subject of financial planning issues behind money to be tedious. Others find it intimidating. As a result, many entrepreneurs avoid it whenever possible. *Financial planning in many businesses becomes the state of the checkbook each morning. If there's cash, the business is still around, and if there's no cash, the business is technically insolvent.*

To be successful, businesses must attend to numbers—including the most important numbers of all, profit and cash flow—closely, diligently and professionally. To be successful, they must sell their goods and services at a profit and satisfy their customers. *There is one simple reason to understand and observe financial planning: to avoid failure!*

Eight of ten new businesses fail primarily because they lack good financial planning. Financial planning affects how and on what terms trade contractors will be able to attract the funding required to establish, maintain, and expand their businesses. Financial planning determines the parts and materials they can afford to buy, the services they will be able to provide, and whether or not they will be able to market their products and business efficiently. It affects the human and physical resources they will be able to acquire to operate their businesses. It is a major determinant of whether or not trade contractors will be able to make their hard work profitable.

A clearly-conceived and well-documented financial plan, the establishment of financial goals, and inclusion of budgets to assure control will demonstrate not only that trade contractors know what they want to do, but more importantly, they know how to do it.

So, let's start Part Two with how to establish a financial plan.

1.0   Financial Planning for the Trade Contractor

The purpose of this standard procedure is to describe the creation of a financial plan, which accompanies the business plan.

2.0   Overview

The financial plan outlines the business's financial objectives in terms of financial and performance ratios, *pro forma* statements (the company's financial reports excluding out-of-the-ordinary transactions), current financing, and capital requirements. Budgets are a required part of this plan along with variance analyses that measures budgeted profits and costs against actual profits and costs (See *Profit and Expense Control*). When drafting a financial plan, keep it concise with supporting material supplied to outsiders like banks and creditors only when requested.

In addition, the financial plan contains *pro forma* financial forecasts. In carrying out the company's action plan for the coming year, these operating forecasts are your guide to business survival and profitability. You include the same information in the annual budget.

Before presenting the company's business plan (see Business Plan) to a lender or investor, review your financial statements with your accounting firm. This familiarity will increase your credibility and at the same time provide you with a good understanding of what the financial statements reveal about the viability of your business. Conducting this review with an outside source increases and hones presentation skills.

3.0   Recommended Financial Plan Format

3.1   Financial Statements. Include the previous years' balance sheet and income statement. An additional two to three years data provides information for trends. Some funding sources require a consistent three year history of profits as well as tax returns for that same period (both company and personal).

3.2   Financial Forecasts

3.2.1   Opening balance sheet for new business divisions or acquisitions.

3.2.2   Projected income statement

❖ This is a month-by-month *pro forma* statement of projected income. It is prepared in conjunction with the twelve month budget prepared each year.

3.2.3   Budget

The budget is prepared month by month for each division and department based upon historical information and the forecast for the upcoming year.

3.2.4   Cash flow forecast (budget of cash in-flow and out-flow on a monthly basis for the next year of operation). This is typically known as the *Statement of Cash Flow*. The numbers from the projected income statement, budget and cash flow must all tie together.

3.3   Financing and Capitalization

3.3.1   Capitalization structure

> ❖ Shows the current capitalization structure as well as the capitalization structure required to achieve the company's financial objectives. Capitalization should reflect a three year time horizon. This also includes funds required for loan or equity infusions. Before and after scenarios (planned and actual) provide insight into the success mode of each operation. Equity offered or loans applied for would include the amount, terms, and when you require the money.

3.3.2   Purpose of loan. Should you require a loan, attach a detailed description of the assets you will finance, with cost quotations and appraisals. A statement of collateral pledged is also usually required.

3.3.3   Owners' equity. This indicates the owners' level of commitment to the program.

3.3.4   Equity or other offering. It includes the funding requirements, investor criteria, as well as the rationale for the equity needed.

EXAMPLE: (See next page)

Building improvements	$3,000,000
Equipment & machinery	750,000
Vehicles	360,000
Non-recurring start-up	120,000
	$4,230,000

Financing

Term loan requested	$1,000,000
Owners Equity	2,100,000
New Investor	2,130,000(10% of company)
	$4,230,000

3.4 Operating Loan

3.4.1 New or increased line of credit applied for, and the security (assets) offered to back the loan.

3.4.2 Maximum operating cash requirement. The amount and timing refer to the cash flow forecast.

3.5 Present financing (if applicable)

3.5.1 Term loans outstanding. Balance owed, repayment terms, purpose of loan, and security held).

3.5.2 Current operating line of credit. Amount and security held.

3.6 Ratios

The important ratios that you need to show include the following:

Liquidity Ratios	Profitability Ratios

Current Ratio	Net Profit Margin
Quick Ratio	Gross Profit Margin
Inventory/Working Capital	Return on Investment (ROI)
Cash Ratio	Return on Equity (ROE)
Productivity of Assets	Earnings per Share (EPS)
Activity Ratios (Annualized)	Leverage Ratios
Inventory Turnover	Debt / Total Assets
Days of Inventory (Days)	Cash Flow / Liabilities
Net Working Capital Turnover	Long-term Debt/Equity
Average Collection Period	Acquisition Interest Coverage
Receivable Turnover	Current Liability / Equity
Cash Turnover (Days)	

Note: It is beyond the purpose of this book to describe and explain the purpose of these ratios. They are best discussed with your company accountant.

3.6.1 Ratios versus Actual

One of the best ways to measure how well the company is really doing is to compare *pro formas* and budgets, with actual performance ratios. Ratios also provide a simple way to determine trends through graphs and charts.

3.7 Breakeven Analysis. Breakeven for a business, division or department is that point in sales volume where direct costs have been recovered, fixed expenses and overhead have been absorbed, and profits begin to accrue. (See *Breakeven Analysis* later in this section for a complete explanation of its meaning). The importance of breakeven lies in the ability to know ahead of time the impact of financial decisions. Breakeven allows a decision maker to determine the *what-if* scenarios of hitting projections as well as the financial effects of missing targets.

3.8   References

❖ Name of present lending institution (address, type of accounts).
❖ Attorney's name (address, telephone number)
❖ Accountant's name (address, telephone number).

4.0   Financial Back-Up Information

You will need the following documents to support a position of growth, expansion, or financial support from outside sources.

4.1   Letters of Intent. Without letters of intent (describing the logic of a new division, product/service line, or acquisition, and its ability to make money), an acquisition's or new division's *pro formas* are not supportable. Letters of intent might also include potential orders, customer commitments, and indications of support. Owners who want to break into new markets should gather these financial back-up documents to make their case.

4.2   List of Inventory. Type of inventory, age, value, and method of valuation.

4.3   List of leasehold Improvements.

4.4   List of fixed assets. Description, age, serial numbers, and similar identification.

4.5   Price lists. This will support cost estimates.

4.6   Description of insurance coverage. Insurance policies, amount of coverage, and type of coverage.

4.7   Accounts receivables summary including customer accounts aging schedule.

4.8   Accounts payable summary including schedule of payments.

4.9   Copies of legal agreements contracts, leases, franchise agreements, mortgages, and other legal documents.

4.10   Appraisals of property and equipment.

4.11   Financial statements for associated companies (where appropriate).

5.0   Organizational Structure

5.1   What is the organizational structure for the financial area? Does it meet the needs of the business?

5.2   Briefly describe who handles what in the financial area. This may be a separate department in a larger trade contracting business or an individual in a smaller business.

5.3   How does information flow and how does management disseminate it throughout the entire company?

6.0   Financial Performance

The surest road to solid financial performance involves:

6.1   Emphasis on quality factors and management actions that lead to improved market performance, market share gain, and customer retention.

6.2   Emphasis on improved productivity, asset utilization, and lower overall operating costs.

6.3   Support for business strategy development and business decisions.

CASH FLOW

As I mentioned previously, cash is the lifeblood of a business. A business needs a steady stream of cash to operate the day-to-day business and meet operating expenses (such as parts and materials, wages, supplies, other overhead expenses, and taxes).

In thirty years of consulting to small companies and many trade contractors, I have found that more businesses sink because they do not understand how to plan for cash to meet everyday operating expenses. This includes companies that shouldn't be on that list because they have plenty of orders, yet find themselves in the predicament of being unable to pay their current bills.

Cash control for any business is essential; for smaller companies that do not have the cash reserves of larger companies, it is crucial.

Trade contractors often confuse cash with profits, but they are two entirely different matters, each calling for special managerial skills. For example, a contracting business may be showing a profit, but in times of inflationary costs or when the business is growing and adding equipment and employees, *it is possible that the business will run out of cash and have to declare bankruptcy.* In this case the skills to manage the business and make it grow are working, but the skills to manage its cash are not.

Suffice it to say that the management of cash—called cash flow—is a skill that trade contractors must address *every day* (that's right, I said *every day*). But it's not difficult. That's why I developed the following procedure for them.

1.0 The Importance of Cash Flow

1.1 The purpose of this standard procedure is to establish a cash flow forecasting methodology that trade contractors can use to project weekly and monthly cash requirements. An effective cash management system is a necessity for optimizing the use of this valuable asset.

1.2 The objective of preparing a cash flow projection is to determine deficiencies or excesses in the cash position, necessary to operate the business for the time period of the projection. If the cash flow analysis reveals deficiencies, management can alter financial plans to increase cash by injecting more equity or loan capital, or by increasing prices, or reducing expenditures.

1.3 In cases where the cash flow analysis reveals excess cash, it might indicate excessive borrowing or idle money that could be "put to work." The objective of cash management is to implement a plan that will provide a well-managed flow of cash.

1.4   The preparation and maintenance of a cash flow forecast requires some time and effort, but the advantage of completing the forecast far outweighs the effort required.

1.5   Cash flow forecasts are more precise over a short term, becoming less precise the further they extend into the future. For this reason, you can get the best results by making frequent cash flow forecasts over the short haul, say, for example, six weeks. As you complete a week and enter actual results, you then project an additional week on the forecast, maintaining a running projection of six weeks of cash flow. You can adjust the length of time over which the forecast extends to encompass the period desired, including as much as one year (prepared through computerized cash flow software).

2.0   Advantages

A cash management system has the following benefits:

2.1   Provides information to evaluate the impact of purchasing decisions before expenditures are committed.

2.2   Facilitates raising additional funds projected for future projects, thereby providing sufficient time to obtain financial support.

2.3   Sharpens awareness of deadlines, particularly those required for tax deposits and other periodic payments.

2.4   Provides checkpoints to compare budgeted against actual results. Significant deviations from the expected results serve as a signal that programs are not moving along as planned. This could mean that plans are not realistic and in need of revision or that management has not foreseen all the pitfalls that create shortages.

2.5   Predicts when and in what quantity dollars will be flowing into and out of the business. The cash flow forecast is a tabulation of company plans expressed in terms of their impact on incoming and outgoing dollar flow.

3.0   Data Collection

The following data should be available from the current financial system to aid in the assembly of the cash flow forecast.

3.1   Sales forecast. This instrument is a projection of sales trends as well as expenditures which have an impact on incoming cash. Each week will require an accurate estimate of cash needed for the period.

3.2   Aged accounts receivable: This document is a schedule of lagging customer payments and displaying performance over time that uncover trends in need of correction.

3.3   Accounts payable aging: All non-operating expense payouts are listed according to their due dates and amounts. For example, taxes, insurance, suppliers, etc. Operating expenses are then projected from current results and past trends.

3.4 Expenditure budgets. This represents historical data of expenses in the business over time, specifically to represent at least one entire business cycle.

4.0 Authority and Responsibility

4.1 Authority and responsibility must be clearly assigned to responsible employees for the specific elements of revenue and cost in the cash flow report. Owners should designate those responsible and assure they maintain confidentiality (normally the trade contractor's accountant).

4.2 Designation of authority and responsibility should specify an individual's role in controlling—for example—payables. Determining which vendors will most easily accommodate stretching payment dates in cash for short periods, and which vendors provide the best advantage to the business for early payment when cash is sufficient.

5.0 Procedure

5.1 Write the forecast in pencil on a thirteen column accountant's worksheet or on a computer spreadsheet.

5.2 Two columns are required for each week, *estimate* and *actual*, and are dated for the *week ending*. Enter the estimate for the upcoming week and the subsequent four weeks. At week's end, enter the actual dollars for comparison to that week's estimate. At the same time estimate an additional week to keep projections out for a period of six weeks. As necessary, make adjustments in the intervening week's cash flow projections based upon experience and performance.

5.3 Line Item Definitions

Cash inflows:

5.3.1 Beginning balance: the amount on hand in bank accounts.

5.3.2 Cash sales: The cash flow into the business from cash sales for the week.

5.3.3 Credit card receipts: Deposits made from charge card sales. Record these deposits in the week when the funds become available to the business.

5.3.4 Line of credit: When applicable, establish a line of credit at the bank to provide working capital in periods of cash shortages. Arrange for the emergency line before the need arises to prevent delays in obtaining cash needed.

5.3.5 **Total cash available**: total of the four elements.

Cash outflows:

5.3.6   Notes or loans payable. Payments made for long and short term loans, notes on equipment, and other payables, including date dues.

5.3.7   Accounts payable. Payments to be made to vendors including vendor names and due dates for major vendors. You can break these out into various descriptive items for each major type of purchase, in keeping with the income statement's chart of accounts.

5.3.8   Payroll. Salaried and hourly wages based upon projected sales revenue of that week.

5.3.9   Payroll taxes. The amount to be paid against payroll. Include the dollar amount in the week in which taxes are paid.

5.3.10   Other taxes. The amount paid against sales taxes and other taxes due. Do not amortize this amount. Include the amount in the week in which you pay the taxes.

5.3.11   Contract services. Amounts due or scheduled to be paid to subcontractors or contract services which support the business.

- ❖ Rent. The amount of monthly rent. Do not amortize this amount. Include the amount in the week in which rent is due.
- ❖ Utilities. Telephone, heat, lights, gas and like accounts. Do not amortize this amount. Include the amount in the week in which the respective utility is due.
- ❖ Supplies. Office supplies which may not be part of a vendor (payable) order. Include the amount in the week in which payment is due.
- ❖ Insurance. Medical, building, equipment, and insurance premiums. Include the amount in the week in which the respective insurance premium is due.
- ❖ Bank charges. Charges for checks, stop payments charges, insufficient funds, line of credit fees, and so on.

❖ Adjustments. Any adjustments to expenses which cannot be accommodated in any of the above expense line items.

5.3.12 Total cash out. All of the items listed above.

5.3.13 **Ending cash balance**. Deduct total expenses from available cash.

6.0 Take Action When *Actual* Differs from *Plan*

6.1 Unless the forecast shows relatively even and healthy cash surplus for each period you will need to make some adjustments to overcome predicted shortages.

6.2 Increased sales can improve the flow of cash, particularly a few weeks into the future. Here's where solid management thinking makes the difference: Managers need to assess whether or not the current cash flow projection is realistic. If it isn't they have to change it. If changes are required, outflow for sales related costs and expenses will have to be adjusted.

6.3 There are times when discounts are available for purchasing in large quantities. It would seem that by taking the discount and buying in volume, the company could earn extra profits. However, there could be a shortfall of cash, and make such a purchase unwise. The cash flow report gives management the tool to help make important decisions such as this.

6.4 You may be able to defer certain payments. Refer to the accounts payable aging report, the schedule of sales related expenses, and operating expenses to determine if this is possible. If so, make the necessary adjustments.

6.5 Adjust payments for capital expenditures to match the cash flow.

6.6 Future liquidity may be enhanced by planning to borrow later. If you take this course, revise both the amount and the timing of borrowing, and the amount of time for debt repayment. *Now, not later, let your banker know of your projected needs. The further in advance the better. The cash flow forecast will give your banker time to suggest alternatives and prepare to meet your needs.* Once the banker has seen your forecasting experience in operation for a few months, the bank will have more confidence in your ability to manage the ups and downs of cash that every company experiences, and have it operate according to the business plan.

7.0 Conclusion

7.1 The cash flow report should be prepared and updated weekly.

7.2   Whoever is responsible for accounts payable should also be accountable for preparing the weekly cash forecast.

7.3   Using a computerized spreadsheet makes this a simple report to prepare and use.

ESTIMATING AND TRACKING

Job estimating is one of the constants in business where trade contractors must submit bids to obtain new orders. The preparation of an accurate, competitive estimate marks the difference between success and failure in many instances, so it is essential that the business owner or estimator be soundly based in the techniques. The estimator's job is to determine and include all anticipated costs incurred to complete a particular job. (See *Bidding Jobs.*)

Job estimates contain six categories:

Material Cost

Labor Cost

Equipment Cost

Other Direct Costs

Overhead

Completed Job Profit

Having estimators who know the particular trade and who understand the numerous aspects of the trade in general is of great importance. Careless or incompetent work in this area can truly cause your business to fail.

Here is a description of the procedure to handle estimating and tracking:

1.0   Purpose

The purpose of this procedure is to provide trade contractor ABC Company with a clearly defined process for estimating new business and tracking what happens to those estimates. These are core functions in the contracting industry because trade contractors often obtain new business through bidding on new jobs. It is important to an effective company operation that those responsible for estimates perform their duties accurately, promptly, and understandably.

The other purpose of this procedure is to explain the most straightforward method of attaining the result of clearly specified cost estimates, bids, and tracking reports.

2.0   Preparing Bids

2.1   A standard organized estimate form is used for estimating any job for ABC.   The form includes:

- ❖ Customer information.
- ❖ Heading information for customer identification and pertinent data along with a job estimate number if available. It also includes references to access, billing, and any other pertinent information.

Section I – Materials Costs

- ❖ Materials – any materials associated with the performance of the job.
- ❖ Considerations for materials:
  - o Listing how much is needed of each material. Do not include specialty items. Also, it is important to nail down specific costs for all materials.
  - o Every item the client will see; in the example of ABC, Inc: doors, glass, tile, wood trim, paint, and primer.
  - o The items the client does not see—nuts & bolts, screws, putty, points, glue, primer, drop cloth, hinges, and other items.
  - o If you're making choices about the grade of materials, address this specifically in your written estimate letter.
  - o For allowances such as specialty materials, make certain it's specifically addressed in your written estimate letter separately from standard materials.
  - o If the customer is supplying any of his own materials make certain that you document this in the written estimate letter.
- ❖ As you are working through the materials portion of the estimate worksheet, markup materials by whatever percentage you think necessary for you to make a profit before calculating the tax amount.   As an example, assuming you markup materials by 20 percent, then:

Actual material costs x 1.20 percent= total material costs including markup. Tax is 8.50%. The tax is calculated as follows:

Total material costs = actual materials costs x 1.20 x 1.0850

Note: Only materials are taxed, never labor or subcontract costs.

Section II – Labor and Subcontractor Costs
Labor

❖ The labor portion of the estimate is broken-out based upon the type of labor required; for example journeyman carpenters, apprentice carpenters, journeyman glaziers, apprentice glaziers, journeyman painters, and apprentice painters. The labor estimate for ABC, Inc. should include considerations for the following labor time as applicable:

  ❖ Estimate of labor time required.
  ❖ Permit acquisition time, if needed.
  ❖ Preparation time.
  ❖ Protection time.
  ❖ Demolition time.
  ❖ Framing
  ❖ Rough inspection time, if needed.
  ❖ Insulation time.
  ❖ Sheet rock, taping, & mudding time.
  ❖ Finish work.
  ❖ Painting time.
  ❖ Clean-up.
  ❖ Final inspection time, if needed.
  ❖ Travel time and shop time.

It is critical that you assess the job carefully so you can identify hours required for each task and each type of laborer required. Use your imagination to think through the job, step by step. Make certain that you identify potential problem areas such as:

  ❖ Insufficient detail in the client's thinking.
  ❖ Structural dilemma.
  ❖ Source of the problem unidentified.

The *actual* labor rate that ABC, Inc. charges per hour has previously considered the following:

  ❖ Employee costs: All those employee costs and labor burden (the costs associated with the employment of the employee over and above the hourly rate. This includes health & welfare, pension, vacation, workers compensation, and employer paid payroll taxes).
  ❖ All those additional costs associated with the performance of the job but not specifically broken out or indirect labor costs. For example driving time, a portion of the

estimation time, a percentage for profit and overhead, and any other non-direct - billable expense.

Overhead

❖ That percentage of total overhead costs, as a percentage of total sales applied to the bid estimate.

Labor Considerations

❖ COLA – cost of living adjustment. If you are involved in estimating a job and your union contract (assuming you have one) allows for a cost of living adjustment, that increases the union employees' hourly rates. You should inquire as to what this percentage is; more specifically, if it is a consideration, and how to apply it.

❖ As with labor planning, take care when estimating for work in other jurisdictions to cover all potential additional costs.

Subcontracting

❖ Subcontracting - This section includes a breakout for subcontracting. In some circumstances, both in-house costs will be calculated and outside bids reviewed from subcontractors, with the most practical and economical selected. The most important issue is to be sure that subcontractor pricing includes taxes on their materials, permits, extras, and contingencies, if any. The cost must portray actual expenditures as closely as possible. Mark up subcontracting costs by XX percent in the estimation after considering all costs (in the materials example shown we used 20 percent). If the subcontractor has hedged the bid in any way, incorporate his assumptions and exclusions into your written estimate letter.

Section III -   Equipment and other considerations
Equipment

❖ Enter any equipment rental or required equipment anticipated. For the ABC example make sure to include ladders, scaffolds, cement mixers, forklifts, dumpsters, tools, special blades – i.e., diamond blades, etc. Obtain all costs of rental including delivery, maintenance, and accessories that may cost extra, late return fees, and taxes. While this generally is not a very large percentage of the total cost, it is certainly worth measuring and worthy of cautious forecasting.

Permits
❖ Drafting fees/filing fees/plans/dump fees. Any additional fees associated with the job.

Travel
❖ Determined by reimbursing standard payment per mile and per diem. As with every other item on the form, you must exercise care in planning to make sure it is an accurate projection.

All of the costs shown above in the ABC example have a 20 percent markup included in the total costs of other equipment or considerations.

Job Costs
❖ To arrive at the calculated job cost, add the total material costs, labor costs, subcontractor costs, and costs of equipment, and other considerations. The price quoted is a result of several factors:
   ❖ What price the company needs to cover its costs.
   ❖ What the competition has or will estimate/bid.
   ❖ How badly does the company want or need the business of a particular buyer or the cash flow from the project?
   ❖ Will the company be awarded the job at the estimated price?

Determining what price to quote is an important skill that borders on an art form. It is beyond the scope of this procedure to attempt a full explanation. It is important, however, to emphasize that sound detailed estimating is essential so there is confidence in the maneuverability from the breakeven point.

3.0 Tracking Estimates or Bid Records
3.1 To have bids that cannot be located or compared to actual costs once a job is completed is a serious lapse in project management. The value of information in making educated management decisions is immense.
3.2 Locate bids by any of the following designations:

A. Job number.

B. Customer name.

C. Type of job performed.

D. Profitability by percent and dollars.

E. Date.

F. Summary of activity.

      G. Awarded or not awarded.

      H. Estimator or bid writer.

3.3 Compare estimates/bids to:

      A. Actual total costs.

      B. Actual labor cost.

      C. Actual material cost.

      D. Actual profitability (percent and dollars).

      E. Actual sub contractor cost.

      F. Actual equipment rental cost.

      G. All other costs.

      H. Actual cost.

With the information available from the reports generated, responsible managers will be able to identify those areas where estimating is off target. Further investigations will reveal reasons for the misses. It will be easier to identify the types of errors that are repeated and by whom. Simply to have such an array of comparative information available opens avenues of understanding otherwise unavailable. *This type of information is a prerequisite for correcting problems and keeping costs within estimated boundaries.*

The next page displays an estimating worksheet for a contractor that designs, chisels, and sells tombstones.

ESTIMATING WORKSHEET FOR A TOMBSTONE CONTRACTOR

LABOR - DESCRIPTION OF WORK	Feet ESTIMATED	LABOR RATE		TOTALS	ACTUAL HOURS	ACTUAL COST		VARIANCE	%
Design-Sq. Ft.	2.00	80.00		160.00	0.00	0.00		160.00	0.00%
Lettering-Sq. Ft.	2.00	80.00		160.00	0.00	0.00		160.00	0.00%
Monument Install-Lin. Ft.	2.50	75.00		187.50	0.00	0.00		187.50	0.00%
Mark.Install-Lin. Ft.	0.00	30.00		0.00	0.00	0.00		0.00	#DIV/0!
	0.00	0.00		0.00	0.00	0.00		0.00	#DIV/0!
	0.00	0.00		0.00	0.00	0.00		0.00	#DIV/0!
TOTAL LABOR			(1)	507.50	0.00	0.00		507.50	

MATERIALS AND SUPPLIES	QUANTITY	COST		TOTALS	ACTUAL QUANTITY	ACTUAL COST		VARIANCE	%
Foundation-Sq.Ft.	2.00	70.00		140.00	0.00	0.00		140.00	
Memorial	1.00	1,097.00		1,097.00	0.00	0.00		1,097.00	
Freight	1.00	65.00		65.00		0.00		65.00	
				0.00		0.00		0.00	
				0.00		0.00		0.00	
				0.00		0.00		0.00	
TOTAL MATERIALS AND SUPPLIES			(2)	1,302.00		0.00		1,302.00	

SUB-CONTRACTOR / OTHER			COST		COST	VARIANCE	%
Foundation			0.00			0.00	
			0.00			0.00	
TOTAL SUB-CONTRACTOR	(3)		0.00		0.00	0.00	

TOTAL PRODUCTION COST (LINES 1 + 2 + 3)	(4)	1,809.50	0.00	1,809.50

					QUOTE	
O/H ABSORPTION RATE	0.33 x LINE 4	(5)	597.14		0.00	LABOR CHARGED FOR
				x	25.00	LABOR RATE
FULL ABSORPTION COST (LINE 4 + LINE 5)		(6)	2,406.64	(i)	0.00	
DESIRED PROFIT	45.55 %	(7)	0.46		0.00	MATERIAL CHARGED FOR
PROFIT : [LINE 7 / (1 - LINE 7)] x LINE 6		(8)	2,013.26	x	0.25	MATERIAL MARK-UP RATE
				(ii)	0.00	
SALES TAX	6.00%	(9)	144.40	(iii)		OTHER CHARGES
QUOTE PRICE (LINE 7 + LINE 8 + LINE 9)		$	4,564.30	(i + ii + iii)	0.00	4,564.30

BREAKEVEN ANALYSIS

A breakeven analysis is a useful financial tool for long range planning. It allows the determination of projected profit or loss and the breakeven point to evaluate changes. Breakeven analysis can help you identify and analyze the anticipated effect of financial actions on cost, revenue, volume, and profit before they are taken.

1.0 The Meaning of *Breakeven*

The ability to calculate the breakeven sales volume provides management with a financial tool that is useful in developing sales and pricing strategies and making decisions regarding capital purchases. The purpose of this standard procedure is to explain the breakeven calculation for ABC, Inc. and to describe some of its applications.

2.0 Definitions

To understand the calculation and its uses some definitions are in order.

2.1 Variable expenses: Those which rise or fall in the same proportion as sales rise or fall. Direct labor and material purchases are variable.

2.2 Fixed expenses: Those which remain relatively the same regardless of the level of sales. Salaries and property taxes are examples of fixed expenses.

2.3 Semi-variable expenses: Those that have elements of both fixed and variable expenses. Payroll taxes are paid on salaries (fixed) and on hourly wages (variable).

2.4 Contribution margin: Sales minus variable expenses.

2.5 Contribution margin percentage: Contribution margin divided by sales.

2.6 Breakeven sales volume: That level of sales which generates a contribution margin large enough to cover all of the company's fixed expenses.

3.0 Breakeven Calculation

3.1 The breakeven sales volume is determined by dividing the fixed expenses by the contribution margin percentage. Stated in formula form, the equation would read:

A.   Sales minus variable expenses = contribution margin.

B.   Contribution margin divided by sales = percentage of contribution margin.

C.   Fixed expenses divided by the contribution margin percent = breakeven sales point in dollars.

For ABC, Inc., using the new 2011 budget as a basis, the calculation is:

Sales	$1,147,019
Variable Expenses	803,644
Contribution Margin	343,375
Contribution Margin %	29.9%
Fixed Expenses	192,557
Breakeven Sales (192,557/0.299)=	$643,222

4.0   Use of the Calculation

4.1   Assume that ABC Company needs a new roofing machine due to heavy sales volume. The cost of the machine is $110,000 including all the bells and whistles. The company would have to generate an additional $367,892 in sales to pay for the cost of the mill. $110,000/0.299 = $367,892.

4.2   A reduction in fixed expenses such as insurance premiums would lower the breakeven and increase profit. Assuming a decrease in insurance premiums of $2,000 the decrease would go straight to the bottom line and the breakeven would be lowered by $6689. ($2000/0.299 = $6689).

4.3   A reduction in variable costs. Improving energy efficiency and reducing utility expenses, for example, will increase the contribution margin and thus lower the breakeven sales volume. Saving $4,000 in utility costs has the following effect. Total variable cost is reduced to $799,644. By our formula the new contribution margin is $347,375 and the contribution margin percent becomes 30.3%. The new breakeven sales volume is $635,501. Therefore a $4,000 reduction in variable cost lowers the sales required to cover the costs of the business by $7,721. From this example you can see that it is worth the time and effort to become a *profit manager*.

5.0   Summary

Contractors can use the breakeven calculation as a financial tool for making decisions on pricing, on purchasing capital equipment. Anything, in fact, involving changes in sales volumes and costs. Since breakeven relates to revenue volume, you can calculate a weekly or monthly breakeven point to establish objectives for the company. *Perform a breakeven analysis at least on a quarterly basis (minimum)* to assure continuing progress toward ABC Company's goals.

BUDGETING AND FORECASTING

As the old saying goes, "If you don't know where you're going you're going to get there before you know it." To put it in our context, "A company that doesn't control expenditures is a company headed for insolvency." Budgeting is a tool that helps trade contractors avoid traveling down that dark road to ruin.

Every company, regardless of how small or how large, needs money for operating expenses to stay in business, and it needs budgets to make sure it contains costs and stays profitable. You can even argue that the smaller company needs tighter budgeting than the larger company does because the larger company often has untapped reserves to draw upon. Most small operators, working on a shoestring budget, such as trade contractors, do not. So every breach is a serious one.

Keeping that in mind, here is a simple, straightforward procedure I developed to help trade contractors budget their operations:

1.0 What Every Company Must Have

1.1   Budgeting is a short-term, detailed plan for running a business or project.

1.2   Owners and managers generally have an idea where they want their business to go, but usually can't steer a straight course there. Unfortunately, the realization they're not heading in the right direction often takes them by surprise. Running over budget on a project is bad, but running over budget and not knowing why spells real trouble.

2.0 Purpose

2.1   Budgeting is the process of making accurate financial projections over a   relatively short term. For ABC Company, this process should take place not only   every year, but should take place quarterly and be monitored monthly.

2.2   Budgeting, in its simplest form, tries to determine exactly how much money will flow in and out of the company and fixes responsibility for specific employees to make it happen.

> ❖ For ABC Company this includes the owners and managers, as well as supervisors and other salaried employees.

2.3   In addition to a fiscal budget, ABC Company should also prepare budgets for each individual project. An individual project budget will:

- ❖ Allow you to take corrective action immediately as conditions change. It provides the ability to act pro-actively before unfavorable changes have taken place.
- ❖ It teaches managers, supervisors, and owners how to effectively manage costs on a project.
- ❖ It provides a mechanism whereby you can evaluate the progress of your managers and supervisors.

2.4   When preparing a budget you try to predict how much money each department will spend and how much you will sell your goods and services for and at what price.

3.0   Financial Forecasting

3.1   Companies use forecasting when they want to know where they stand financially and where they're going—how they will close out the month or year with respect to profit and cash flow. Forecasting is simply a detailed estimate of where the business financial momentum will carry it over a certain short period.

3.2   If the forecast yields an unsatisfactory result, you can sometimes take short term actions to achieve your objectives. For example, if revenues for the month look as though they will be somewhat short of projections, you can react by loading the current schedule with work normally scheduled for next month to make up the shortfall.

3.3   Forecasting is especially important with respect to cash requirements. If a company is to pay its bills and make its payroll, management needs an accurate picture of the cash they expect to come in and go out over the next few weeks and months. If they predict a temporary shortage, a relationship with a bank has to be set up to keep the firm running until collections catch up with disbursements.

The typical trade contractor will work with his accountant to establish and maintain budgets. It is beyond the scope of this book to describe the various budgeting methods that are best for individual trade contractors (they vary and must be custom-tailored for every business). But it is the responsibility of the trade contractor to track progress or lack of it to his company's budget, detect variances early before they have had a chance to materially affect projected company profit, and take appropriate corrective actions to eliminate the variances.

PROFIT AND EXPENSE CONTROL

There isn't a commercial company in existence that doesn't need a rigorous profit and expense control procedure to guide its daily operations if it expects to succeed and flourish. Profit and expense control is a system for establishing standards and allowable expenses that will produce predetermined profits at specific levels of revenue activity. It provides a road map for the company to assure it maintains forecasted profit levels as revenues and costs change. I have found the following procedure to be especially effective in helping trade contactors hold projected profit and expenses to budgeted amounts.

1.0   The Importance of Expense Control
    1.1   This procedure provides a road map for ABC Company as a basis for understanding the steps in establishing control and maintaining standards for allowable expenses. The object is to forecast, track, and control predetermined profits at specific income levels.
    1.2   All business activities are divided into major categories of income and expenses:
        1.2.1   Sales.
        1.2.2   Cost of Goods Sold (for an integrated trade contractor manufacturing part of his supplies).
- Material purchased (variable expenses).
- Direct labor service and installation hours (variable expenses).
- Service and installation parts (variable expenses).

        1.2.3   Cost of Business Operations
- Selling expenses.
- General & administrative expenses.

        1.2.4   Profits
    1.3   The objective of the system is to limit the controllable expenses to the amount needed to support the income generated and report them in a way that will allow management of ABC Company to (1) monitor the activities of the company on a monthly basis, (2) determine the variances from planned results, and (3) take corrective action in the shortest possible time when expenses exceed budgeted amounts.

1.4   The control system is also a measuring device or management tool enabling measurement of, and evaluation of, key employees, as well allowing key employees to evaluate themselves.

2.0   Objective

2.1   The objective of a profit and expense control system is to control expenses so that *income* less *profit* will offset the operating expenses incurred.   Of course, in a technical sense, profit is the first expense of business. Management needs to consider it as a fixed dollar amount; otherwise slippage is inevitable.

3.0   Advantages of Controls

3.1   The advantages of using a control system are as follows:

❖ It has strong influence on the most economical use of working capital since its object is to make the maximum use of facilities and assets.

❖ It prevents waste since it regulates the spending of money for a definite purpose and in accordance with a preplanned program (budget).

❖ It requires coordination as it compels cooperation among all employees to obtain results planned in the budget.

❖ It presents preplanned expenditures that are committed to a definite business purpose and consistent with profit goals.

❖ It acts as a safety device for management because it indicates variances from the standards established. The object is *no surprises!* By checking variances in the short term it prevents deficits in the long term as management is in a better position to apply corrective action and head off losses.

❖ It compels management to study and plan for the most economical use of labor, materials, and equipment.

❖ It establishes a target of performance and provides a gauge for measuring results.   Thus, it is a test of management's ability to make things happen in accordance with a well-ordered plan.

4.0   Development of Profit and Expense Tools

4.1   Refer to the chart *Profit and Expense Flow Overview* at the end of this section.   It represents in graphical form the interrelationship of the activities and procedures used to establish financial control of ABC Company's business.

4.2   The chart of accounts must be structured to separate accounts related to the company's services and overhead expenses by profit center.   This is done to emphasize areas of expense control and responsibility. A management chart of accounts will also closely resemble the business' income statement format.

4.3   An historical income and expense review and seasonal sales analysis will define sales highs and lows in the fiscal year and determine what annual and monthly sales and expense goals are reasonable and within reach. These are developed and maintained by whoever is in charge of sales in conjunction with the company bookkeeper.

4.4   The annual budget is then projected from the data and analysis performed in section 4.3 above. The annual budget for each sales and expense category is then developed as a part of an annual business planning cycle.

4.5   The flexible, or variable, budget, a concept that ties budgeted accounts to the sales volume, is generated from the annual budget and the monthly sales projections. The flexible budget concept has the following attributes:

- ❖ Simplicity of operation.
- ❖ Flexibility to allow for fluctuations in levels of business activity.
- ❖ Effectiveness of control.
- ❖ Sets clear objectives in dollars for controlling costs.
- ❖ Provides management with a tool for measuring actual performance versus planned or budget requirements.
- ❖ Provides management with the tools for assigning expense and cost accountability to the responsible parties.

4.6   When actual sales for the month have been determined, management can use the flexible budget to generate the adjusted budget for that month. These adjusted budget numbers are entered into the budget section of a variance report along with actual cost and expenses. The variance report will then indicate the difference between actual and the adjusted budget in terms of both dollar and percentage variations.

4.7   In addition, the report displays year-to-date variations. Managers can analyze the variance report to determine what costs are out of control and need immediate attention, and also what parts of the budget need tweaking to make it more accurate.

4.8   Unfavorable variances must be explained by those who are accountable, and a target deadline set for a written plan on how the variances will be avoided in the future.

5.0   Extension of Control

5.1   If desired (and this is highly recommended), top management should extend the process to each manager and supervisor by giving him responsibility for the areas of the budget under his control.

5.2   Managers and supervisors can then be accountable for keeping their budgeted accounts under control.

5.3   When the budgets are allocated to each manager's profit/cost center, the control to a budgeted level will be a major measurement tool for each manager's performance.

The chart displayed below (*Profit and Expense Flow Overview*) illustrates the relationships described in this section.

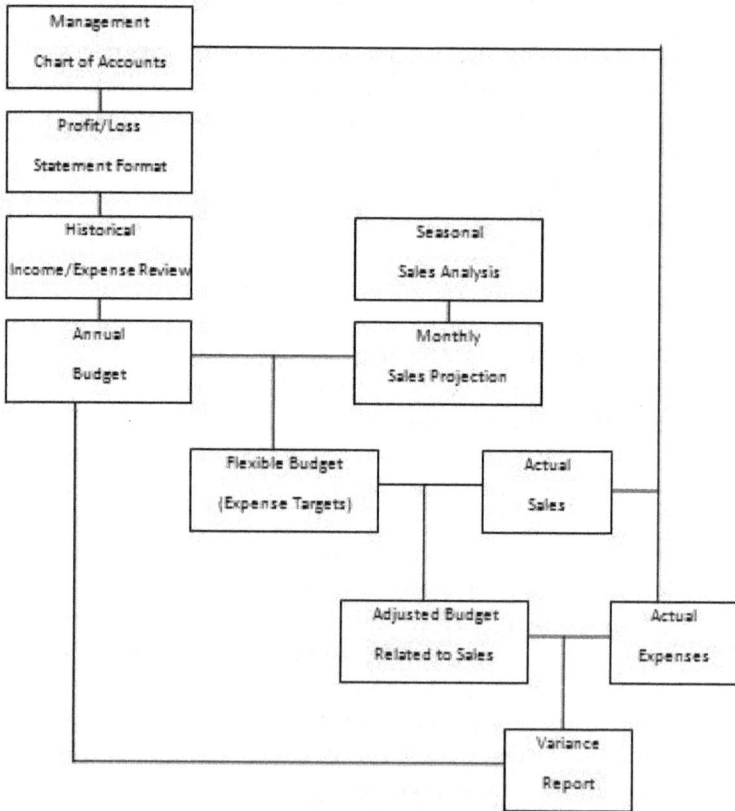

ACCOUNTS RECEIVABLES AND COLLECTIONS

The purpose of this standard procedure is to outline the method by which a trade contractor (1) determines whether to grant a customer credit, (2) determines how much credit to grant, and (3) handles its account receivables after it extends credit to customers. Following such a method minimizes bad debt and interest expense, improves cash flow, and increases interest income.

1.0   One of the Main Reasons for Financial Failure

1.1   A typical aspect of many businesses is that a company invests or ties-up a large percentage of its limited financial resources in the receivables created by credit sales. Credit sales are a two edged sword: the sword cuts favorably as well as unfavorably. On the one hand, extending credit enhances sales by attracting customers that may otherwise be lost if credit is unavailable. Conversely, careless or nonexistent control over account receivables results in scarce cash tied up in slow paying accounts, unnecessary losses from bad debt, and the need for additional financing. It can, and has, resulted in bankruptcies.

1.2   Owners and managers of the trade contractor's business should view accounts receivable as a *so near, yet so far near-cash asset*. **A credit sale is not really a sale until the company collects the account,** regardless of its disposition under the accrual basis of accounting. **Prior to collection, the only tangible outcome that a credit sale produces is a financial burden straining cash resources.**

1.3   Accounts receivable is a very expensive asset. Payment for services rendered have not been received, but expenses for salaries, supplies, equipment, and overhead have been incurred and probably already paid.

1.4   Most of this operating procedure focuses on the fundamentals of a good collection policy, although collection policy is just one of the three main activities of credit policy (See *2.0 Credit Policy*).

1.5   Designing and maintaining an effective collection policy is not a simple task. The policy must strike a delicate balance between generating the pressure needed to obtain payment from delinquent accounts and offending customers.

2.0   Credit Policy

The essence of the management of accounts receivable is a good, clearly articulated and understood credit policy. The credit policy consists of three elements or activities:

2.1   The decision on granting credit and the terms offered the customer.

- Obviously the first component of this is the credit application. With this document, you ask for sufficient information to make the determination whether the applicant is credit worthy or not. It should be completed, reviewed, and approved before granting credit. *The Credit Application must be obtained in sufficient time to be approved before granting credit.*

There are several components vital to this element of credit policy:

- The president of the trade contracting company is responsible for the overall application of credit policy.
- The sales representatives ask for and receive completed credit applications; then, they forward them to the credit manager (in a small operation this person is likely to wear several hats, probably for all administrative tasks) who has oversight responsibility to assure that the application is completed and received on every new account.
- The credit manager verifies all information on the credit application.
- The credit manager calls and checks all references given on the application.
- The approval of an applicant as *credit worthy* is a joint decision made by the president and the credit manager before partial or full payment is due.
- The credit manager notifies the customer that he's approved the credit application . . . first, by a phone call and then by a follow-up letter.
- The next important component is the terms offered the customer.
- The third step is the collection follow up and begins *the very first day* that an account becomes past due. More on this later in Section 5.0.

2.2   The monitoring of account receivables to control the funds tied up in this asset.   An accounts receivable aging report must be generated at least weekly so that all accounts can be reviewed, and delinquent accounts identified early enough to initiate timely and effective collection proceedings.

2.3   The formulation and execution of an effective collection policy. This activity is as crucial to sound credit management as the first two. Regardless of how carefully credit applicants are screened, a firm is likely to have delinquent accounts and experience bad debt loss. But an effective collection effort minimizes losses. It can shrink the length of delinquent periods.

3.0   Essentials of the Collection Procedure

3.1   In order for the collection procedure to work effectively, you must have the following:

- ❖ A correctly aged listing of account receivables.
- ❖ One designated person with the authority and the credibility to collect account receivables, and still maintain the best possible client relations. This means collecting the monies due without offending the customer.
- ❖ A record of collection efforts for each account. The collection follow-up record (one record for each contact—this is not a log) is prepared when collection activity becomes necessary. Here's an example:

Table 1 - Collection Follow-Up Record

Client Information Name, Address, Telephone No.	Date of Contact	Time of Contact	Person Contacted	Conversation	Payment Action Promised

You can maintain a collection follow-up record using either 3X5 or 5X8 index cards or a Microsoft Excel list on your computer.

- ❖ Maintain these contact records in a tickler file (a file that reminds the user of matters that must be attended to and when) to determine future action needed.   Organize the tickler file in a fashion resembling the following:

o   The first section has an index for every day of the month (day 1 - 31), and is used for actions during the current month.

o   The second section has a file for all twelve months and is used for follow up accounts not scheduled for the current month. At the beginning of each month, open these records and re-file them according to scheduled follow up data.

o   The third section is an alpha (a - z) section for the collection records of accounts that are now closed. This permits a quick credit and collection follow-up review on clients' return visits.

3.2   Work with the tickler file on a weekly basis.

❖   Open the collection follow up records.

❖   Review the records to see if customers have made payments.

❖   Initiate follow up action as indicated.

❖   A word about files. There is no standard method for setting up the files. The person responsible for collections should have it organized so there is a logical order to it so that anyone can use them to see which accounts are delinquent.

4.0   Using the Telephone to Collect Receivables

4.1   There are many valid reasons to use the telephone to collect accounts receivables.

4.1.1   There may be valid reasons why a customer did not pay on time. Sending an impersonal form letter or a bill with *Past Due* stamped on it to a good or long time customer will not help public relations. The personal touch can do much in maintaining a good relationship with the customer. A phone conversation with the customer will help him reach the right decision for both involved parties.

4.1.2   The customer knows, in no uncertain terms, that you are on top of things. You contacted a delinquent account promptly and did not let the problem go unattended.

4.1.3   Telephone calls are the most inexpensive and inoffensive means to establish communication and collect the money from a customer. It can also be the source of information for determining the exact nature of the problem, why the customer is delinquent, and feedback regarding the overall financial health of the customer for consideration of future orders.

    4.1.4   A telephone call is effective because it establishes direct contact between two people to mutually and honestly discuss the delinquent payment of an invoice.

    4.1.5   During a telephone call, you control the discussion, you get the answers you are seeking, you can be flexible in your approach, and you can be thorough, personable, and persistent.

4.2   Prepare thoroughly for the telephone call before.

    4.2.1   Have the customer's contact name correct in spelling, title, and (perhaps most importantly) pronunciation.

    4.2.2   Have all the pertinent information about the account and the amount in question directly in front of you so you can readily and easily answer any questions the customer has.

5.0   The Collection Process

5.1   The first steps

    5.1.1   The collection effort begins at the time that the company performs services. At the time of the sale, you need to clearly explain the company's accounts receivables policies.

    5.1.2   The second step begins with the mailing of the invoice.

    5.1.3   The third step is the collection follow up and begins *the very first day* that an account becomes past due.

5.2   The gentle reminder

    5.2.1   Phone immediately after the account becomes *one day past due*. Your credit terms may be, for example, 2%/10 days, net 30. Therefore, you place the first reminder phone call on the 31st day.

> ❖ During this call to the client contact responsible for payment, you must clearly establish that the account is overdue and delinquent.
>
> ❖ Determine if there is any problem with the work performed or with the product.
>
> ❖ If there were any problems, establish if they were resolved to the satisfaction of the customer.
>
> ❖ Be polite, be firm, and ask for payment, then note what promises the customer made on the collection follow up record.

❖ After this telephone call, send the customer a first collection letter (Form A/R 1 as shown on the pages at the end of this section).

❖ On the third business day after a promised date for the check to arrive and it doesn't, place a second call to the responsible party and indicate that the promised check has not arrived. Note the results on the collection follow up record.

❖ After this second telephone call, send the customer the next collection letter (Form A/R 2 as shown on the pages at the end of this section).

❖ The polite but firm phase will now escalate to the next phase.

5.3   The demand phase

5.3.1   Enter this phase after the second attempt to collect the receivable fails.

5.3.2   This phase is also the final stage of your in-house collection effort. This is the customer's last chance to settle the account before you turn it over to either a collection agency or a lawyer to recover the aged receivable.

5.3.3   In this phase, it may be appropriate for the manager of the person making the initial two contacts to get involved for a more forceful collection effort.

5.3.4   The telephone conversation in this phase, while polite, is short, to the point and firm—*very firm*.

5.3.5   Occasionally, the mention of legal or outside collection sources is all it takes to convince the customer that you really are determined to collect your money.

5.3.6   Record the results of the conversation on the collections follow up record.

5.3.7   After this telephone call, mail the third follow up letter (Form A/R 3 as shown on the pages at the end of this section).

5.4   At this point in the process, you have two choices:

5.4.1   Turn the receivable over to either a collection agency or a law firm specializing in the collection of delinquent accounts; or,

5.4.2   Send a letter making one last demand for the payment. Keep in mind that if this alternative is used, this is truly the last chance for the customer. Should the letter fail to prompt payment, turn the account over to an outside collection resource.

6.0   Some Games People Play
6.1   There are several ways in which some clients may delay or avoid meeting financial obligations.

6.1.1   Postdating the checks.

6.1.2   Sending the checks unsigned.

6.1.3   Sending a partial payment, but writing *Paid in Full* on the check or on the statement's remittance note.

6.1.4   Altering the check or the billing statement in such a way that it will require additional time for re-processing.

6.1.5   Asking questions about the invoice and requesting more and more information faxed or mailed before the invoice can be processed.

7.0   Some Additional Thoughts on the Collection Process
7.1   Don't use phony tactics; tell the customer the exact reason for the contact and exactly what you expect.

7.2   Do not in any way threaten the customer.

7.3   Do not embarrass the customer.

7.4   Do not argue with the customer.

7.5   Never apologize for calling and never appear hesitant about demanding payment. It is, after all, your money.

7.6   Always assure that the customers make a firm commitment about when he intends to submit the payment.

7.7   When you tell a customer that you are going to take a certain action—whether it is to send a copy or something, or to turn the matter over to a collection agency—*you absolutely must do it.* To not do so is equivalent to sending a message to the customer that your demand for payment is not serious.

8.0   Summary
8.1   The foundation of a collection policy should be clear, effective communication between the trade contractor and its customers. This communication begins with the customer's application for credit, and continues through all subsequent contact with the customer. The emphasis of this communication is the customer's responsibility as a recipient of credit, and the firm's responsibilities as creditor. *Avoid the necessity of sending an account to a collection agency by assuring you have a clearly articulated credit policy, and by letting all customers know what the policy is and that you expect compliance.*

8.2   Have the new customer complete a credit application and evaluate it *before extending credit*, or assure that you have gathered enough information to check the new customer's credit rating through D&B or some other credit reporting agency.

   8.3 Telephone calls are the primary collection tools. The key questions are who, when, and how much.

   8.4 Complete the collection follow up reports without fail.

   8.5 The person responsible for collection activity must always act in a businesslike, professional manner, and never allow the customer to take advantage of the company.

   8.6 It is worth noting that while generalizing human behavior is difficult and tricky, there is one common train of which informed creditors are well aware: a debtor who shuns communication and fails to respond to telephone or mail contact is invariably either unwilling or unable to pay. In cases like this, do not wait until the account is 60 days old to take vigorous action.

   The following three pages display fill-in-the-blanks forms you can send to customers delinquent in paying their bills.

Form A/R 1

Dear :

The purpose of this letter is to confirm our telephone conversation on the date shown above regarding our invoice number _____ dated __ _____, and in the amount of $_____.

During our conversation, you indicated that you will be sending your check to cover the full amount of this invoice on _____.   Based on this date, I expect to receive your check no later than _____.

Thank you for your prompt attention to this matter.

Sincerely,

Form A/R 2

Dear :

The purpose of this letter is to confirm our telephone conversation on the date shown above regarding our invoice number _____ dated _ _____, and in the amount of $_____.   You indicated in our conversation today that you will be forwarding a check for the full amount of this invoice on _____.

Recalling our previous conversation of _____,   you made a similar arrangement, but you were not able to meet that obligation. Your prompt attention to this overdue invoice is appreciated. Based on your promise to pay, we expect the check by _____.

Sincerely,

Form A/R 3

Dear :

Today was our third telephone conversation regarding your past due payment on our invoice number _____ dated _____, and in the amount of $_. We expect full payment of this seriously overdue invoice to be in our office no later than _____.

We value our relationship with you and your company; however, we will have to consider other action for collection of this past due account if the check does not arrive in our office by the date shown above.

Effective today, you are on C.O.D. basis and credit privileges have been suspended until such time as your account is paid in full.

Sincerely,

WHAT YOU NEED TO KNOW ABOUT ACCOUNTING

Accounting is the measuring stick of the company. It helps trade contractors make the right decisions regarding where to apply the company's limited financial resources. Without an accounting system the company owners would not know if their business is profitable or losing money. Therefore, it stands to reason, that company owners and managers must understand at least enough about accounting systems to know if it's doing its job and accurately reporting all costs of the business.

1.0 Purpose

1.1 This operating procedure on accounting will not make you an accountant, but it will provide a basic understanding of some accounting terms, principles, and reports. This basic explanation will at least provide you with an idea of what it takes to accurately portray the financial affairs of a business.

1.2 We highly recommend that you continue your business relationship with your accountant. He will be able to provide you with valuable assistance regarding the state of your financial reports and supply guidance on establishing and maintaining a good working relationship with your business partner, the Internal Revenue Service (IRS).

2.0 The Accounting Entity

2.1 Your company is an accounting entity. As your accountant will tell you, it is important that you keep the accounts of your company separate from your own personal accounts.

2.2 The accounts are expressed in dollars, and the only math used in accounting is addition and subtraction.

2.3 The common denominator for all accounting is dollars.

2.4 Accounting can't tell you everything about your company, but it can tell you more about its performance and financial well-being than any other source of information.

3.0 Accounting Concepts to Remember

3.1 There are three important concepts to keep in mind about accounting. They are:

3.1.1 Maintain accounting records of your business separate from your personal affairs.

3.1.2 Dollars are the common denominator of accounting.

3.1.3 Every transaction or every accounting event affects at least two items, a debit and a credit. That's why accounting is truly a double-entry system.

3.2 The third rule just described leads to the following rule, to which there is absolutely no exception: *For each transaction the debit amount must equal the credit amount.*

3.3 The debit and credit arrangement used in accounting provides a useful means of checking the accuracy of recorded transactions. Some say that this is a difficult notion to understand, especially if you don't have a background in, or have never taken a course in accounting, but don't worry about it.

3.4 When you make entries into your accounting software, the debits and credits will be transparent (and will do all the work for you).

4.0 Accounting Reports to Remember

4.1 The two main end products of an accounting system are:

4.1.1 Income statement (also called the profit and loss statement).

4.1.2 Balance sheet.

4.2 The Income statement measures your company's financial performance for a period of time, called an accounting period. You will probably spend more time with your income statement than with your balance sheet.

4.3 The Balance sheet reports your company's financial status at a specific point in time.

5.0 The Balance Sheet

5.1 The balance sheet is a snapshot of the financial condition of your company at a specific date. It is always dated at a given point (day, month, and year) in time, while the income statement states that it covers a certain period of time.

5.2 The balance sheet has two sides.

5.2.1 The one on the left side is the assets side. Assets are resources owned by the company.

5.2.2 The one on the right is the equity side. Think of equity as either claims against the assets (liabilities), or the amount of funds which have been invested in the company from various sources (equity).

5.3   The **fundamental accounting equation** is: **Assets = Equity** (often called **Liabilities**). The double entry principle of accounting is based on this equation.

6.0   Debits and Credits

6.1   Debits and credits provide a very convenient way of applying the principle of double entry. They describe how *increases* and *decreases* are reflected in the chart of accounts (a listing of all the different asset and liability accounts in the general ledger).

6.2   There is another accounting equation to go along with the fundamental one described above, that is, **Debits = Credits.**

The rules which apply to debits and credits are:

6.2.1   An asset is increased by a debit and decreased by a credit.

6.2.2   A liability or equity is increased by a credit and decreased by a debit.

7.0   Income Measurement by the Income Statement

7.1   Being a profit-oriented company, your success is reflected by positive changes in the equity section of the balance sheet. The equity section will increase by the amount of the profit your company makes. Since the balance sheet is a snapshot, you can see only that equity has changed but you can't determine why it changed.

7.2   That's where the income statement plays such an important role. Here you see exactly what your revenues and expenses were and how they affected your bottom line. Very simply, the income statement shows the detail of why retained earnings (an equity account) changed.

8.0   Explanations of Accounting Terms

8.1   **Assets:** The assets of a business are everything of value held by the business. The word value as used here means future usefulness to a continuing business enterprise. Cash, notes, and account receivables (amounts owed to the business by customers), land, buildings, and high-grade, readily marketable stocks, or bonds of other companies are examples of assets in a business. An asset is recorded on the books of the acquiring entity at actual full cost, even though it has not been fully paid for in cash (referred to as the cost principle). The amount of any debt or claim against the asset is included in the liabilities.

8.2   **Equities:** Equities are claims against the total assets of a business. The two major classifications of individuals who have equities in a business are creditors (the liability holders) and owners. A business's liabilities are owed to its creditors.

8.3 **Liabilities:** These are the debts or claims of creditors against the assets of the business. Accounts payable, notes payable, and wages owed to employees are examples of liabilities.

8.4 **Owner's equity:** This is the owner's claims against business assets. It is also called **Net Worth** and is the excess of total assets over total liabilities. Because creditor claims have priority over the claims of the owner of the company, owner's equity claims are secondary (or residual).

8.5 **The Balance Sheet:** It is an expanded expression of the accounting equation, **Assets = Liabilities + Owner's Equity**. It summarizes the assets, liabilities, and owner's equity of a business entity as of a specific point in time. Another name for the balance sheet is **Statement of Financial Position**.

8.6 **Current Assets:** They consist of cash and other assets expected to be converted into cash or to be used in the operation of the business within one year. Current assets are usually listed in descending order of their expected conversion into cash (liquidity).

8.6.1 Cash: Any item that a bank will accept as a deposit and that is immediately available and acceptable as a means of payment.

8.6.2 Accounts Receivable: Amounts due from customers for services rendered, for merchandise, or for any asset sold on credit.

8.6.3 Notes Receivable: Formal written promises to pay a fixed amount of money at a future date. Most notes can usually be exchanged for cash at a bank.

8.6.4 Merchandise Inventory: Products on hand and for sale. This type of inventory is found on retail store shelves and in stockrooms or warehouses.

8.6.5 Prepaid Items: Services and supplies acquired that will be consumed during the next 12 months. These are classified as assets because they are items of value that have future usefulness in business operations. Some examples of prepaid items are:

❖ Prepaid Insurance: Businesses take out insurance policies for protection against hazards. The cost of this type of protection, an insurance premium, is paid in advance. The unexpired portion of the prepaid insurance premium is an asset.

❖ Office Supplies: Supplies such as stamps, stationery, and business forms required in an office and grouped under the title office supplies are current assets of the business.

8.7 **Property, Plant and Equipment:** This classification consists of assets used over a long period in the operation of a business. They are customarily listed on the balance sheet according to their degree of permanence, with the most permanent item listed first.

8.7.1 Land: Always listed separately. Although land and the buildings on the land are usually sold together, they are classified separately because the buildings will deteriorate through usage, whereas the land will not. Land is considered the most permanent asset.

8.7.2 Buildings: Those owned by the business appear on the balance sheet. Rented buildings are not owned and are not included as assets.

8.7.3 Store Equipment: Showcases, counters, and shelves are typical permanent items of store equipment used in selling the merchandise inventory.

8.7.4 Delivery Equipment: Consists of trucks, cars, and other types of equipment owned and used for the delivery of products to customers.

8.8 **Current Liabilities:** This term designates obligations whose liquidation (in other words: payment or settlement) is reasonably expected to require the use of current assets or the creation of other current liabilities. All liabilities to be paid within a one-year period are classified as current. They are generally listed in their probable order of liquidation.

8.8.1 Accounts Payable: Purchases on credit. They are the unpaid amounts owed to creditors from purchases on an account arrangement. They are usually due to be paid within 30 days and are also called open accounts.

8.8.2 Notes Payable: Formal written promises by the company to pay money to creditors. Trade notes payable derive from the purchases of merchandise or services used in the course of business. Notes payable to a bank arise when a company borrows money for business use.

8.8.3 Accrued Liabilities: Since the word accrue means to increase by growth or to accumulate in a standard manner, accrued liabilities are debts that have accumulated because of the passage of time that are not yet due for payment. Accrued wages payable and accrued interest payable are typical examples of accrued liabilities.

9.0   Conclusion

9.1   This accounting primer is a much abbreviated introduction to accounting.

9.2   Your accountant can provide you with greater detail, and The Business Doctor (that's me) will provide you with assistance in getting management reports and information.

10.0   Glossary of Accounting Terms

Account: A recording device used for sorting accounting information into similar groupings.

Accounts payable: Amounts which the company owes to creditors for purchases made.

Accounts receivable: Amounts due from customers for sale of goods or services to them.

Accrued: Accumulated over a period of time.

Accrual basis of accounting: The assumption that revenue is realized at the time of the sale of goods or services, regardless of when customers pay their bills. Expenses are recognized at the time the services are received and utilized, or an asset is consumed in the production of revenue, regardless of when payment for these services or assets is made.

Asset: Something of known value owned by the company.

Balance: The difference between the total of debits and credits in an account.

Balance sheet: The financial statement which summarizes the assets, liabilities and equities of a company. The stated value reflects worth at a specific date.

Budget: A financial plan for a period of time, normally a month, quarter, or year.

Cash: Currency, coins, traveler's checks, checks, and any other items that your bank will accept for deposit.

Chart of accounts: A list of all accounts in the general ledger which the company anticipates using.

Credit: The right side of the T-form of an account, the actual amount on the right side of an account, or the act of placing an amount on the right side of an account.

Creditors: Persons or companies to whom the company owes money.

Current assets: Cash and other assets that will be either consumed or converted into cash within twelve months.

Current liabilities: Liabilities which will be paid within twelve months.

Debit: The left side of the T-form of an account, the actual amount on the left side of an account, or the act of placing an amount on the left side of an account.

Disbursement: An actual payment by cash or check.

Double-entry accounting: A system of recording both the debit and credit aspect of each transaction.

Entity: Your company—separate from you as an individual.

Equities: Claims against the total assets of a business.

Expense: Expired cost; the material used and service utilized in the production of revenue during the specific period.

Fixed expense or cost: An expense or cost that remains the same total amount over the short run and does not vary with changes in sales volume or sales revenue. Over the longer run, these expenses and costs are raised or lowered as the business grows or declines. Fixed operating costs provide the capacity to carry on operations and make sales.

Gross profit or margin: Equals sales revenue for a period less total cost of goods and services sold for the period *and* equals profit before the deduction of operating expenses, interest, and income tax expenses.

Inventory: The stock of products held by a company either for conversion into products for sale to customers or for immediate sale to customers.

Liability: The obligation of a company, or a creditor's claim against the assets of a company.

Long-term liabilities: Debts of a company which are not due within the current year.

Matching concept: An accounting principle which reflects the matching of incurred expenses and earned revenue for a given time period in order to determine net income for that period.

Mortgage payable: A debt, normally long-term, for which specific assets such as a building are pledged as securities.

Net assets: Total assets less total liabilities.

Notes payable: Short-term notes to creditors, much more formal than accounts payable.

Overhead: For trade contractors, this refers to indirect operating expenses. Indirect means that the expense or cost cannot be matched or coupled in any obvious or objective manner with particular products or specific revenue sources.

Owner's equity: The owner's claim against the assets of the company.

Prepaid Items: Unconsumed amounts of current assets not normally used in the current operations of the firm, and that are not held for resale.

Property, plant and equipment: Long-lived or long-term assets of a company that are used in the operations of the firm and are not held for resale.

Transaction: A business activity or event which has taken place.

Trial balance: A statement that shows the name and balance of all ledger accounts arranged according to whether they are debits or credits. The total of the debits must equal the total of the credits in this statement.

PART THREE

ASSURING THE BUSINESS SURVIVES AND FLOURISHES: MAJOR RESPONSIBILITIES AT THE TOP OF THE COMPANY

In this section we will examine the responsibilities of the owners and top managers of the trade contracting business. Specifically:

The owners' responsibilities

The board of director's responsibilities

The president's responsibilities

Strategic planning

The business plan

The succession plan

Company policy: what it covers

THE OWNERS' RESPONSIBILITIES

1.0 The Owners' Responsibilities

1.1 The owners provide capital for the corporation and establish the basic direction for the company. They collectively determine major goals and policies, and delegate day to day decision-making to the president at least to the extent described below.

2.0 Reporting Relationships

2.1 The president is elected by the board of directors.

2.2 The board of directors is elected by the stockholders (owners).

3.0 Authority

The owners are authorized to:

3.1 Establish the company's general direction and policies.

3.2 Establish goals for the company in sales, gross profit, and operating profit.

3.3 Approve all investments, acquisitions, and long-term financing plans for the company.

3.4 Approve all spending for capital expenditures.

3.5 Approve all actions of the president above that position's defined limits of authority.

4.0 The Owners' Responsibilities Defined

The owners have the primary responsibility for setting direction and policy for the company. They:

4.1 Meet at least once per year for a shareholders' meeting, and function as a corporation as required by law.

4.2 Provide goals for the company that guide the company's direction.

4.3 Monitor the performance of the company to assure it meets the owners' objectives.

4.4 Select the top management team.

4.5 Are responsive to other stakeholders in the company besides the owners:

4.5.1 Customers, who expect product quality and efficient service.

4.5.2   Employees who make the company operate efficiently and rely on the company for their livelihood.

4.5.3   The community-at-large, which benefits from the company's jobs and services.

4.5.4   Suppliers, who profit from doing business with the company.

5.0   Principal Duties

The owners have the following duties:

5.1   Charter the business and comply with all applicable federal, state, and local laws regarding corporations.

5.2   Establish the company mission and basic company policies. Direct the president to communicate these corporate guidelines to all employees.

5.3   Determine the length of office for the president. Provide an evaluation of the president and determine that position's compensation level.

5.4   Establish company standards for customer service, quality, and safety. Monitor operations to assure that the company's employees meet expected performance in line with company goals (See *Business Plan*).

5.5   Review and approve all capital expenditures.

5.6   Meet annually to review and update the strategic plan.

5.7   Meet annually to set one-year financial goals for such areas as:

- ❖ Net operating profit.
- ❖ Return on investment.
- ❖ Debt to equity ratio.
- ❖ Sales goals.
- ❖ Growth.
- ❖ Investment opportunities.
- ❖ Capital investment.

5.8   Additionally, company owners perform any other duty required to fulfill the responsibilities of ownership or to serve the best interests of the company.

THE BOARD OF DIRECTOR'S RESPONSIBILITIES

1.0 The Board of Director's Responsibilities

1.1   The purpose of this position guide is to establish and define the functional role, relationship, and responsibilities of the board of directors.

2.0 Functions

2.1   The board of directors shall meet a minimum of one time per year to elect the president. The president shall notify the board of directors as to the time and place of the meeting.

2.2   The board of directors shall notify the stockholders as to the condition of the company a minimum of once per year.

2.3   The board of directors shall provide ongoing support and expertise to the president, assisting him in establishing goals, objectives, policies, and procedures for all revenue dependent systems in the company.

3.0 Reporting Relationships

3.1   The board of directors reports to the stockholders.

3.2   The president reports to the board of directors.

4.0 Responsibilities of the Board Defined

4.1   Provide guidance, counsel, and direction to the president.

4.2   Establish annual company financial and operating goals.

4.3   Establish long range objectives so that the company can proceed toward these goals and objectives.

4.4   Develop company growth strategies and objectives through the development of new markets, diversification, or acquisitions.

4.5   Assure capital is sufficient to support all operations.

4.6   Review the annual budget.

4.7   Review and approve all capital expenditures over a given amount as determined by company policy.

4.8   Perform any other duties that are in the best interest of the company.

THE PRESIDENT'S RESPONSIBILITIES

1.0 The President's Responsibilities

1.1   This procedure outlines the basic function, position requirements, reporting relationships, authority, responsibilities, and measures of performance for the president of the company.

1.2   What's contained in this procedure is not designed to be the job description of the president, but rather to provide a thinking piece for the development of the president's job description.

Note: In the smaller company the president may wear many hats. But when performing other duties, the president must take care to assure that presidential functions take priority.

2.0   Basic Functions

2.1   The president is responsible for the overall profitable operations of the company.

2.2   The primary function of the president is to oversee the operations of the company, to assure compliance with all of the company's policies and procedures, and to take the necessary remedial steps when he finds areas of non-compliance.

2.3   The secondary function of the president is to provide the necessary supervisory leadership to plan, organize, direct, coordinate, and control the activities of all employees reporting to this position and thus ensuring the business operates within the budget.

3.0 Reporting Relationships

3.1   The president, by virtue of his ownership, reports to the stockholders and indirectly to the customers.

3.2   The president has direct authority over the following:

    3.2.1   Operations function (field superintendent).

    3.2.2   Controller function.

    3.2.3   Sales function.

In the smaller company the operations manager and sales manager may be the same employee.

4.0   Authority

By virtue of his leadership position, the president has complete authority over all aspects of the business.

5.0 Responsibilities of the President Defined

5.1   To hire, dismiss, and change the duties and compensation of the positions answering to the president.

5.2   To approve any developed operating procedures and policies.

5.3   To negotiate and approve contractual agreements with lenders for capital loans or lines of credit, and approve all final agreements committing the company to any on-going financial agreements.

5.4   Legal and prescribed responsibilities:

5.4.1   Assure that the performance and operation of the company is in compliance with all pertinent governmental laws, rules, and regulations.

5.4.2   Assure the prudent operation of the business.

5.4.3   Review the proper and complete handling of all legal matters.

5.4.4   Review the proper and complete handling of audits, financing, market share, and growth.

6.0 Tasks and Duties

The duties and tasks of the president shall include but not be limited to the following:

6.1   Assure that the responsibilities of each employee are accompanied by the corresponding authority equal to the task of fulfilling those responsibilities.

6.2   Assure the maintenance of a functional company by:

6.2.1   Making use of job descriptions.

6.2.2   Making use of the organizational chart.

6.2.3   Taking growth and shrinkage of sales and orders into account.

6.3   Assuring that decision making is decentralized and performed at the proper levels.

6.4   Company Relationships

6.4.1   The president is responsible for relationships with all managers.

- ❖ He must be ready to render assistance where necessary.
- ❖ He must coordinate all required communications across the company.
- ❖ He may delegate all or part of these responsibilities along with the corresponding authority.

6.4.2   The president is responsible for the public and professional image of the company.

6.5   Organization and employees

6.5.1   The president is responsible for developing an organization to meet the needs of the company, and update them as necessary to   accommodate changing conditions.

6.5.2   The president is responsible for establishing job descriptions for each key position and hiring qualified people to fill each position.

6.5.3   On a semi-annual basis, as a minimum, he must conduct a performance evaluation on the positions reporting to his office. The president must also review the performance evaluations of all the employees evaluated by the other managers.

6.5.4   The president is responsible for reviewing any disciplinary actions taken by the managers to assure both legal compliance and fairness and consistency in application of discipline.

6.6   Financial Responsibilities

6.6.1   The president must review and monitor the financial controls for safeguarding the assets of the company, and examine fiscal performance. This includes assuring that an efficient and effective accounting system is in place and maintained.

6.6.2   The president must monitor the operations of the business through verbal and written communications on a regular basis, assuring that all operations are running according to budget and plans.

6.6.3   The president must review the financial needs, obligations, and action plans of the company as well as the company's stature and integrity in the community.

6.6.4   The president is responsible for authorizing, approving, and maintaining sufficient insurance to protect and preserve the assets of the company.

6.6.5   The president is responsible for reviewing the company's accounts receivables, assuring that bad debts do not exceed the budgeted annual goal.

6.6.6   The president must review and approve the annual budget prior to each fiscal year.   As well as approve monthly budgets and follow up on variances at the end of each month.

6.6.7   The president must review the pricing of the products and services   provided by the company to meet both sales projections and profit margins.

6.6.8 The president must review inventories on a constant basis to assure profitability.

6.7   Planning and Evaluation

6.7.1   Along with the company's senior managers, the president must establish a three-year strategic business plan, and review the ongoing efforts of the company to meet its long-range goals.

6.7.2   He is responsible for negotiating, accepting, or approving all major contracts to which the company will become a part of, such as loans,   leases,   mergers,   acquisitions,   labor contracts, customer contracts,   and   real   estate   or   capital purchases.

6.7.3   The president must select, secure, and coordinate all legal, accounting, banking, consulting, and other professional services that are deemed necessary for the protection and promotion of the assets of the company.

6.8   Operational Responsibilities

6.8.1   The president must assure that the company complies with all federal, state, and local laws, ordinances, rules, regulations, and statutory requirements to minimize the liability of the company.

6.8.2   The president must operate the company in a profitable manner, assuring a reasonable rate of return on invested dollars.

6.8.3   The   president   must   maintain   open communication and a harmonious working relationship with all employees, but in particular with those   involved   in   a   direct reporting relationship.

6.8.4   The president must personally resolve all business and human relations problems or grievances not satisfactorily settled by managers.

7.0 Measures of Performance

The board of directors evaluates the president's performance. The yardsticks are:

7.1   The amount of profit contributed to the company by all sections of the business. This includes the company staying within the annual budget.

7.2   The state of morale and spirit of cooperation within the company, including the degree of cooperation, communication, and coordination between managers and employees.

7.3   Meeting or exceeding the company's goals and objectives, including foremost, sales and profit goals.

7.4   Demonstrating the capacity and ability to establish and maintain the organizational stability of the company.

STRATEGIC PLANNING

Strategic planning creates a road map of the company's future. Company owners set a general direction for the company through goals for the planning horizon, normally five years, although the time frame varies. Succession planning (See *Succession Planning*) is one example of the owners' goals. This general direction sets the stage for operating managers who flesh out the plans with specific action goals.

Here's how it works: Top management comes together, normally through a series of meetings, and devises goals for the immediate year as well as for the next few years. The company president reviews and makes changes or approves the goals to assure they meet the owners' interests. These become the strategic plan, identifying the path ahead for the company.

The strategic plan includes forecasting major capital improvements as well as changes in normal operations. Financial planning ties both factors together in a funding plan. After the plans are set, management develops an operating budget which anticipates revenues and costs by categories. (See *Budgeting and Forecasting*). The operational and financial planning provide backup to bankers for required borrowing.

The planning team develops timelines for each step to achieve stated goals. By participating in goal setting, managers and supervisors learn to understand what the owners want, provide knowledgeable input based on their hands-on experience, and draw up plans of action.

Through strategic planning, the company considers the risks and opportunities it faces, and identifies ways of meeting them. This proactive approach provides the company with flexibility. Altering a plan already in place as conditions change is easier than developing new plans from scratch to overcome every obstacle.

Benefits of strategic planning:
- ❖ Encourages disciplined thinking about the business.
- ❖ Explores key threats and opportunities.
- ❖ Builds a systems perspective about the whole operation.
- ❖ Reduces fire-fighting and crisis management.

- ❖ Outlines financial needs and helps secure bank loans.
- ❖ Provides measurable performance objectives.
- ❖ Improves communication and commitment in the management ranks,

Here is a time-tested procedure for strategic planning:

1.0   Start with Gathering Information

1.1   This procedure is designed to provide the outline and initiate the gathering of necessary information to develop a strategic plan for the company. Note: Any plan is only as good as the effort and commitment that employees put into it.

2.0   Functions

2.1   Managing is the way in which organizations accomplish their objectives. It is the method by which they get things done. Strategic planning is the method that determines what things need to be done. It provides the goals and objectives of the business.

2.2   Without strategic planning, a company is operating without clear purpose and direction. Decisions made without regard to company goals and objectives do nothing more than detract from performance resulting in a waste of assets, capital, and employee effort.

2.3   Strategic planning and goal setting are essential parts of every business. A plan of action fleshes out the strategic plan with definitive goals and objectives so that the work effort and resources are directed in a controlled and coordinated manner.

2.4   An effective strategic plan establishes achievable goals and objectives. Good managers and supervisors manage their businesses every day without losing sight of goals and objectives. They make decisions and changes as required to keep the business progressing toward its present goals and objectives.

2.5   Without a plan, a business tends to run on historical experience or by crisis management. Managers reach in different directions due to lack of clear, common goals. This creates confusion, inefficiency, excessive costs, and lost profits.

2.6   The lack of a plan also limits growth. Its substitute, day-by-day management, doesn't account for contingencies. Essentially, you are flying blind. Although businesses cannot plan for all contingencies, planning will reduce risk and will also provide guidelines for staying on course.

3.0 The Basic Process

3.1   The first part of the process is to develop an accurate assessment of the company's capabilities and the depth of its employees. This involves the gathering of information from within the company and evaluation of the skill and ability of its employees. The purpose of this is to examine the company's state. What is its condition? How capable are its employees? What assets are available? What are its weak points?

3.2   The second part of the process involves an examination of factors outside the company. These are things which can affect success of the plan and are not under the control of the company. Government regulations, for example. What about new technology and the new product lines they generate? You need to answers these questions along with others related to the proposed plan.

4.0   Outline for the Strategic Plan

4.1   A company's **Mission Statement** (See *Mission Statement*) narrowly limits its intended purpose and should be considered a point of orientation, like a guidepost. It is the company's reason for existing and carefully defines the business. For example: *To provide economical products for customers in our expanding area. To address the special needs and interests of our customers. To provide a safe and professional environment in which to work, stressing growth of employee skills and keeping pace with changing customer demands.*

4.2   **Strategies** are specific methods that will be used to accomplish the goals. For example: Develop a process for reporting hours from the field or assign goals for field employees to work more efficiently. Strategies are the *how* of the plan.

4.3   **Action steps** are the step-by-step plan of how to accomplish stated goals. It assigns needed assets, authority, and responsibility, along with a timetable including completion and reporting dates. This assures the plan moves forward and goals are achieved. There are no excuses because everything necessary for the plan is provided for.

4.4   **Long range goals** are usually written for a period of three years. Management must ask itself the following:

- ❖ Where do we want to be in the long range as we have defined it?
- ❖ What profit levels can we reasonably expect to achieve?
- ❖ What resources do we need to achieve stated goals?
- ❖ At what time periods will we need the resources?
- ❖ How will we finance the plan? What are the capital requirements?
- ❖ What are our profit goals and profit strategy?

4.5   **Market forces** are carefully analyzed to determine and categorize those factors that will generate demand for the company's services now and in the future. The area of marketing can be examined in a business plan, but a separate comprehensive marketing plan is also helpful and in cases of intense competition, essential (See *Part Six: Marketing Trade Contractor Services*). This is market segmentation and is useful because it may:

❖ Uncover previously overlooked markets.

❖ Be helpful in deciding where to concentrate the company's increased sales efforts.

❖ Identify specific new target markets.

After identifying the market segments, the next step is to make a decision to target individual segments. Using a *What If?* scenario, determine the effects of such matters as potential decline and potential increases in sales and what the company must do to meet its goals in these market segments.

4.6   **Market potential** is reviewed across the company's total potential markets to determine how the company can effectively service them with its existing capacity. This includes plans for increasing the company's percentage of the market. After determining the market objectives for each of the three years of the plans, you then formulate plans for the employees, facilities, and financial requirements needed to support projected growth. Questions to explore are:

❖ Do we have enough employees available to support the growth or will we have to increase the staff? If we increase staff, from where will they come? Are our compensation programs competitive? What training is required?

❖ Do we have the facilities and space to support the volume forecast? What additions or replacements will be required? What new or expanded facilities will be required?

❖ What are the cash requirements necessary to support projected growth? Will major capital expenditures be required? Will long term borrowing be necessary? Is it available? At what costs? How will cost-of-living factor affect our costs?

4.7   **Competition awareness** is as important as knowing your company. Know your competitor's strengths and weaknesses, market share, geographic coverage, and everything else you can discover. A *competitors' library* is useful information to compile. In it, one should maintain such things as competitive services offered, market share, pricing structure, their reputations in the marketplace, financial strength, and so on. You can obtain additional information through trade associations, chambers of commerce, trade journals, Dunn & Bradstreet Reports, and other compiled and reported business analyses. Here are some examples of information to collect and monitor:

- ❖ Company locations and sizes.
- ❖ Cash resources.
- ❖ Advertising materials.
- ❖ New markets into which competitors are moving.
- ❖ Quality of service.
- ❖ Service capabilities.
- ❖ Pricing and bidding strategies.
- ❖ How competitors promote themselves (methods and approaches).

4.8 Form M-100A (*Setting Goals and Objectives*) at the end of this section, is a worksheet used to document applicable goals and objectives. The form is only a guide which can be expanded becoming more specific based on what the company plans to accomplish.

4.9 Form M-100B (*Goal Planning Sheet*) which follows Form M-100A is a form to be used once goals are established. Give this form to employees responsible for achieving goals and ask them to complete the form. Once complete, return those completed forms to the supervisor who reviews it with the employee and approves the plan. Then return a copy of the form to the employee responsible for achieving the goal. Supervisors then periodically check to determine progress.

5.0   Implementation, Measurement, and Follow-Up

5.1 When you complete your basic analysis, of factors both within and outside the company, it is time to put the plan in writing. With goals now defined it is time to start the process. Take these following steps:

- ❖ Write a detailed plan.
- ❖ Assign a plan administrator.
- ❖ Prepare a master calendar with deadlines for all associated tasks.
- ❖ Assign assets, authority, and responsibility for individual tasks.
- ❖ Review, evaluate, and take corrective action or implement changes as determined by events.

❖ Monitor progress or lack of it with reports and meetings as necessary.

❖ When goals are achieved, start new strategic plans.

5.2 Failure to achieve a specific goal or action step requires reviewing the plan. Learn from your efforts and make corrections which improve your planning abilities. Here are typical reasons for missed goals:

❖ The goal may have been wrong.

❖ Poor effort or execution.

❖ Wrong timing.

❖ Conditions may have changed.

❖ Wrong strategy.

❖ Inadequate assets assigned to the task.

6.0   Summary

6.1 Use the guidelines described above for constructing goals and objectives and melding them into a strategic plan. A well developed three year plan will take a lot of effort and commitment to write.

Form M-100A

SETTING GOALS AND OBJECTIVES

By:_____Date:_____

A. Review
1. What business are we in?
2. What business do we want to be in?
3. What services do we currently offer?
4. Why do our customers buy our products and services?
5. On a scale of 1 to 10, with 10 being the highest, how would our customers rate us? Why?
6. What are we doing right?
7. What are our strengths:
    ❖ As we see them?
    ❖ As our customer sees them?
    ❖ As our competitor sees them?
8. What is our target market?
9. What is our market share?
10. Who and what is our competition? List the strengths and weaknesses of the top three.
11. Did we grow in the past year? What factors contributed to the growth or lack of growth?
12. What portion of our business is produced by each type of service we provide?
13. What portion of our profit is produced by each of these services?
14. Which expenses have increased as a percent of sales over the last three years?
15. Which expenses have decreased as a percentage of sales over the last three years?
16. What equipment do we have? Do we need more? Less?
17. At the current levels of compensation and training, what is the capacity of the current staff?
18. What is the capacity of our current facility?

B. Looking to the Future

1. What are our revenue goals:
   - ❖   2012 _____ 2013 _____ 2014 _____
2. What is our revenue strategy:
   - ❖   Projected increases will come partially from an inflationary increase of: _____percent   ($_____)
   - ❖   Projected increases will come partially from expanding the customer base and new types of business (list the amount from each).
   - ❖   List other anticipated expenses.
3. What is our employee strategy (additional workforce required).

Year	Management	Supervisors	Workers
Year 1	_____	_____	_____
Year 2	_____	_____	_____
Year 3	_____	_____	_____
Total	_____	_____	_____

4. What is our facilities and equipment strategy?

   A. Present facilities (will/will not), and equipment (will/ will not) be adequate to accomplish goals.

   B. Additional funds of $ _____ will be required for facilities through Year 1.

   C. Additional funds of $ _____ will be required for equipment through Year 2.

   D. Additional funds of $ _____ will be required for equipment through Year 3.

   E. What dollars will be required for:
   Year One: $ _____ Year Two: $ _____Year Three: $ _____
   Improvements: _____ Improvements: _____ Improvements:_____
   F. What improved facilities will be required for:
   Year One: $ _____ Year Two: $ _____Year Three: $ _____
   Improvements: _____ Improvements: _____ Improvements:_____
   G. What new equipment will be required for:
   Year One: $ _____ Year Two: $ _____Year Three: $ _____
   Improvements: _____ Improvements: _____ Improvements:_____

5. The source of funds needed to finance projected costs and expenses will be produced from:

	Profit	Bank Loans	Personal	Other
Year 1:	$_____	$ _____	$ _____	$ _____
Year 2:	$_____	$ _____	$ _____	$ _____
Year 3:	$_____	$ _____	$ _____	$ _____

6. Profit goals (projected net profit before tax)
   Year 1 $ _____   _____ %

Year 2 $ _____   _____ %
Year 3 $ _____   _____ %

7. Profit strategy:
❖ Reorganize and establish management control of operations through
        Delegation (_____ %)   Accountability (_____ %)
        Evaluation (_____ %)   Training   (_____ %).
❖ Pre-control expenses to accommodate profits (_____ %).
❖ Provide different services to increase customer base (____%)

8. Business expansion planning:
❖ New ventures and product lines
        Annual revenue potential: $ _____
❖ List of equipment and facilities that will be required:
❖ Anticipated capital expenditures: $ _____
❖ Labor requirements: $ _____

	Number	Estimated Annual Labor Costs
New employees: _____		Year 1 $_____
Year 1 $_____	Year 1 $_____	
Managers: _____$__		

9. What are the industry, technological, and environmental trends likely to affect us in:
❖ One Year?
❖ Two years?

10. What government regulations or restrictions will affect us in:
❖ One Year?
❖ Two Years?
❖ Three Years?

11. What factors will aid our growth in the future?

12. Is there anything else we need to consider? Is there an employees' agenda not contemplated in the questions we have asked so far?

Form M-100B

GOAL PLANNING WORKSHEET

Name: _____ Department: _____ Date: _____

Define or Describe Goal:

_____
_____
_____
_____
_____

Describe the plan to attain:

_____
_____
_____
_____
_____

What is the present position relative to the goal?

_____
_____
_____
_____
_____

What is the time frame for completion?

_____
_____

Describe the expected specific benefit or result:

_____
_____
_____
_____
_____

List any specific obstacles:

_____

_____

_____

_____

_____

What are the plans for overcoming obstacles:

_____

_____

BUSINESS PLANNING

Any trade contractor either starting a new business or expanding his existing business is best served by committing his plans to paper (or a digital file). This process is called *business planning* and it involves laying out a roadmap of what the owner expects from the business in the future.

Unfortunately, most trade contractors don't take the time to write down their business plans and, instead, rely on memory. But memory will only take you so far, and chances are day-to-day concerns will soon swamp your memory banks and you will forget important aspects of the business plan that often spell the difference between success and failure.

Writing a business plan forces the trade contractor to think through his strengths and weaknesses and evolve a business plan that plays to his company's strengths. It will help him better understand the market and his customers' expectations and his ability to meet them.

With that in mind, let's examine the business planning cycle.

1.0 The Critical Nature of Business Plans

1.1   Business planning is the science of bringing together all of the resources of the trade contractor for planning operations, specifically maneuvering forces into the most advantageous positions prior to taking action.

1.2   It is important when considering this procedure that your thinking adheres closely to this definition of strategy because it will help you to specifically define your business activities and your company's future direction.

1.3   Careful design of a business plan allows you to respond appropriately to business conditions and opportunities, to meet specific objectives, and to avoid many unpleasant surprises down the road.

1.4   Business planning determines the difference between mediocre and excellent sales and profit. That is why you are here, isn't it?

2.0   The Planning Process

2.1   The business planning cycle is constant, whether the plan is being designed to affect the entire business operation or to assist in making a single decision affecting only one part of the business.   2.2   Stages in the cycle are:
- ❖ Review the current situation.
- ❖ Establish the revised objective.

❖ Define the factors affecting the plan.
❖ Establish the strategies needed to reach the objective (develop a *Business Action Plan (BAP):* the plan that will achieve the stated goals).
❖ Review your strategies to accomplish the plan.
❖ Implement the Business Action Plan.
❖ Review progress periodically and, if necessary, modify the objective, the BAP or both to reflect changing conditions.

3.0   Review the Current Situation

3.1   Establish the current condition of the company. In other words, take a present day snapshot.

3.2   Briefly, take stock of your present situation regarding all areas of operation, for example:
❖ Market environment.
❖ Products and services.
❖ Pricing and profitability.
❖ Customers (who they are and what their needs are).
❖ Administration and management requirements.
❖ Financial resources.

3.3   Keep this report to one page.

4.0   Set the Objective

4.1   The objective(s) should be:
❖ **Appropriate.** They ring true for what you expect to be doing.
❖ **Acceptable.** They fall within accepted industry and political norms.
❖ **Feasible.** They permit appropriate and timely response to contingencies.
❖ **Measurable Over Time.** They are able to be monitored and controlled over time periods extending perhaps a number of years.
❖ **Motivational.** They are aggressive yet achievable and within reach so employees are encouraged to accomplish them.
❖ **Understandable.** They make sense to others not familiar with your concepts such as bankers.

4.2   Try to assure that objectives are zero-based, not extrapolated from past trends or current budgets. Point them to the future without reference to past or present conditions.

4.3   Make your Objectives read as a simple **statement of intent**, for example:

❖ To increase customer base by 15 percent during 2012.
❖ To establish a new asphalting facility in 2013.
❖ To train and develop and train a back-up field manager by the end of 2012.
❖ To achieve a 10 percent increase in asphalting capacity during the next fiscal year.

4.4   Note that your objective can be as wide or as narrow in scope as you want it to be. Regardless, *the business planning process does not change!*

5.0   Assess the Factors Likely to Affect Your Plan

5.1   Factors likely to affect your planning can include virtually anything: the weather, political influences, environmental considerations, the economic climate, or simply time, among others.

5.2   It is important that you give full rein to your imagination at this stage. Think laterally and try to list all of the external factors (those which are not within your capacity to control) which may have an impact on your business or long term personal plans.

5.3   What you are trying to do is establish *best case/worst case* scenarios in order to eliminate surprises that will interfere with achieving the stated objective(s).

6.0   Develop the Business Action Plan

6.1   The Business Action Plan must include:

❖ A written statement of the objective.
❖ A brief review of the current position.
❖ A summary of factors affecting the plan.
❖ A detailed, written strategy designed to achieve the objective, in essence a step-by-step how-to manual.
❖ A record of who will be accountable for performing each step of the plan.
❖ A schedule for implementation of the plan specifying check point dates or other monitoring devices.
❖ A notation on the action to be taken, by whom, in the event that unforeseen circumstances interfere with the smooth implementation of the plan at any stage.
❖ A summary of review procedures to be used, and a definition of the parameters which will be applied to determine successful completion of the plan.

6.2   The objective you set will determine the scope of the Business Action Plan. Planning can be made on a global scale for the entire business operation or on a micro scale addressing one single issue. A full business plan will likely address the following issues:

❖ Management and staffing.
❖ Product and service descriptions.
❖ Market analysis.
❖ Market strategies.
❖ Financial projections including:
   o Twelve month flexible budget schedules.
   o Three, five, or 10 year income projections.
   o Cash flow projections for the same periods.
   o *Pro forma* balance sheets.
   o A breakeven analysis.
   o A sources and uses of funds statement.
   o Capital expenditure budgets.
   o Financing requirements analysis.
   o Investment decisions and schedules.

6.3   Note that the lists above are guidelines only. There may be any number of other issues or topics that you will want to include in your planning, and consideration must be given to *all* factors pertinent to your objective.

6.4   Make each strategy a statement of imperative action. The strategy statement should serve to both impel action by those who will be implementing the strategy and to motivate them to see that your strategy succeeds. HINT: Start each strategy statement with an action verb. Make them positive and not negative in context.

7.0   Review Your Strategies

7.1   Before implementing your action plan it will be necessary to review the strategies you have designed to assure their validity.

7.2   Use the business review checklist (shown at the end of this section) as a guide to the conduct of this review process. It contains some, but probably not all, of the review criteria which you may want to apply.

7.3   If your Business Action Plan fails this review you will need to re-think elements of the plan itself or perhaps even redefine the original objective, then repeat this review process.

8.0   Implement the Business Action Plan

8.1   Take the necessary action to put your Business Action Plan into effect. Do this step by step according to defined schedules and monitoring check points that you have established for your plan.

8.2   Remember that this is a *business plan* and not a New Year's resolution. You will have spent considerable time, effort, and likely money, to design the plan so don't waste it by ignoring the end result and proceeding as if it didn't exist. Here's the bottom line: **Your plan must be followed to be effective!**

9.0   Review Progress and Results

9.1   The degree of progress towards your objective must be measured on a regular and continuing basis according to the review, and monitoring should be according to the review and monitoring criteria established.

9.2   In some instances you will review your plan almost daily. In other instances you may want to review progress quarterly, semi-annually, or even annually. The review periods will be determined by the nature of the plan, its criticality to operations, and its exposure to variable influences.

9.3   Progress reviews may be carried out in some cases by the company owner alone. In others, a project review committee composed of all or some of the management team will be established and will hold regular, formal review meetings. Again, the nature and scope of the plan will determine your course of action, but whatever the circumstances, the *review must be carried out as specified in the Business Action Plan.*

9.4   The progress review may result in modifications to the original Business Action Plan. This is acceptable; remember that your plan should be flexible enough to respond to changing conditions. However, it is important to assure that any modifications to the Business Action Plan or to the original objective be treated with the same methodical care as the original plan itself. Follow all the steps in the planning process when designing modifications to the original Business Action Plan.

10.0 Evaluation Criteria

The list below represents some, but not all, of the fact-finding consideration that should be included when analyzing and evaluating the present condition of the company, the setting of objectives and the design of strategies.

❖   What business are we in?
❖   What products or services do we currently offer?
❖   What is our target market?
❖   Why do our customers do business with us?
❖   On a scale of one to 10, with 10 being the highest, how would our customers rate us? Why?

- ❖ What is our market share?
- ❖ Who is our competition? List the strengths and weaknesses of the top three.
- ❖ What are our strengths?
  - o As we see them.
  - o As our customers see them.
  - o As our competitors see them.
- ❖ What are our weaknesses?
  - o As we see them.
  - o As our customers see them.
  - o As our competitors see them.
- ❖ What is our current organizational structure?
- ❖ Did we grow in the past year? What factors contributed to the growth (or lack of growth)?
- ❖ What portion of our business is produced by each product type or service?
- ❖ What portion of our profit is produced by each product type or service?
- ❖ Are all our products or services profitable? If not, why are holding onto them?
- ❖ Which expenses have increased as a percent of sales over the last three years?
- ❖ Which expenses have decreased as a percent of sales over the last three years?
- ❖ What portion of sales is produced in each month for each product type or service?
- ❖ At current levels of compensation and training, what is the capacity of the current staff?
- ❖ What equipment do we have now?
- ❖ What is the capacity of the equipment we have? Do we need more? Less?
- ❖ What is the capacity of our current facilities?
- ❖ What are the industry, technological, and environmental trends that are likely to affect us over the next:
  - o One year?
  - o Three years?
  - o Five years?
- ❖ What government regulations or restrictions will affect us in the next:
  - o One year?
  - o Three years?

- o   Five years?
- ❖ What are the economic trends that will affect us in the next:
  - o   One year?
  - o   Three years?
  - o   Five years?
- ❖ What factors will aid our growth in the future?
- ❖ What factors will limit our growth in future?
- ❖ Where do we want to be in:
  - o   One year?
  - o   Three years?
  - o   Five years?
- ❖ Is there anything else we need to consider? Is there a personal agenda not contemplated in the questions we have asked so far?

BUSINESS REVIEW CHECKLIST

❖ **Verify** that all strategies define means to achieve the objective you set. If they merely restate the objective, modify or reject them.

❖ **Verify** that your strategies are consistent with an analysis of the market place, your capabilities, and your resources.

❖ **Assure** that the return on investment (ROI) is sufficient to justify the risks.

❖ **Assure** that your strategies are consistent with the political environment within your company.

❖ **Assure** that your strategies are based on facts and not on assumptions or a wish list.

❖ **Examine** whether your strategies leave you critically vulnerable to sudden shifts in the market environment. Are all your eggs in one basket?

❖ **Examine** your appraisal of the competition. Is it open-minded and honest?

❖ **Make Sure** your strategy is legal. Are you *absolutely* sure?

❖ **Examine** whether the success of your strategy is based on your ability to sustain it. What are the chances of failure? Do you need specialized assistance to succeed?

❖ **Assure** that you have carefully examined all identifiable alternative strategies before accepting the one you selected.

❖ **Verify** that a sound deductive rationale exists for your business, strategy, or recommendations.

SUCCESSION PLANNING

A closely held corporation, such as most trade contracting businesses, needs a succession plan just as much as any other type of business. Stockholders and executives of a closely held corporation are usually one and the same. When a stockholder dies, the corporation, unlike a partnership, continues its independent legal existence. The deceased stockholder's shares are passed on to his heirs. If the owner made no plans for the sale of stock or for a management change, the death or retirement of a major stockholder could cause a host of problems for the business, the surviving shareholders, and the heirs.

If the surviving shareholders own a majority of the stock, control of the business isn't affected. However, the business may sustain financial losses when the expertise of a key manager is lost. The heirs of a minority stockholder may complicate business affairs since heirs have the right to vote and demand information about the management and finances of the company.

These are just some of the possibilities a business may face if it is stranded without leadership in key functional areas. Consequences are serious, so it is important for any type of business to have a succession plan.

1.0 Don't Be Caught Without a Succession Plan

The succession plan requires that owners consider many factors prior to the development of the actual legal documents. The purpose of this standard procedure is to list those factors.

2.0 Considerations

- ❖ Retirement age of owner(s).
- ❖ Monthly and annual income needs.
- ❖ Investment plans if any.
- ❖ Tax ramifications to the owner.
  - o Estate Taxes
  - o State Taxes
  - o Federal Taxes
- ❖ Possible methods of succession
  - o Sell to relatives.
  - o Sell to existing partners.

o Sell to employees.
o Sell to outside individual.
o Sell to an established corporation.

3.0 Potential Financing Arrangements

❖ The owner accepts payment of a specific amount. A new buyer will pay a specific amount a month for a stated number of years. The owner retains partner status in the business until payments are completed.

❖ Relatives begin a buy-in and over a specific time purchases 100 percent of the stock.

❖ The partner buys-out other partners by purchasing additional shares of the company each year.

❖ Employees buy-out the company under an employee's stock ownership (ESOP) plan.

❖ A corporation purchases the business. The owner receives his entire payment in a lump share. The ownership is transferred immediately.

4.0 Professional Assistance

❖ Consult with your C.P.A. to determine all tax ramifications in various types of ownership transfers or in an outright sale.

❖ Seek and use legal advice in succession plans to avoid pitfalls.

5.0 Timetable

❖ Develop a plan to remove yourself from the business as stated in your personal objectives. The timetable establishes the time frame over which you plan withdrawal.

❖ The way to accomplish this is to establish a reduction of involvement with the business through delegation and follow-up by taking the date one wishes to be completely withdrawn, and withdrawing over a period of time, say 2-3 days per week for six months, than 3-4 days per week for the next six months, than 4-5 days per week the next six months until you've accomplished a full withdrawal from the business.

❖ Establish outside interests that you develop over this period of time that are substituted for the previous time spent in the business. *If it's time for retirement, beware of developing interests that cannot be walked away from; otherwise you're tied to the new interests. You want to be able to do what you want to do, when you want to* (within reason and with agreement of the spouse of course).

6.0 Summary

The idea is to plan for retirement so that there is no sudden change and the feeling of loss does not have an impact on your daily schedule.

MISSION STATEMENT

The mission statement is a document many trade contractors overlook in their preoccupation with technical matters and the rush and pressure of everyday business. It helps when formulating the mission statement, or any of the other documents listed in Part Three, to "get away from it all" to have time to think and plan. Perhaps the owner and his staff can spend a long weekend at a local hotel or the owner's home and really give serious thought to the direction of the business.

1.0   Purpose of the Mission Statement

1.1   A mission statement can be the foundation from which a trade contractor establishes policies and procedures. This standard procedure explains the method of formulating a simplified corporate mission statement used as a communication device with employees and the public.

While it is true that the larger the contracting business the more a formalized procedure such as this applies, it is also true that even the smallest trade contracting business can benefit by the type of direction it provides for its owners and managers.

2.0   Concept

2.1   A mission statement communicates to employees the company's overall expectations, direction, and focus (See also *Strategic Planning, Business Planning*). Company owners and managers develop goals, policies and procedures within the confines set   forth   by   the   mission statement. The basic function of a mission statement is to convey to the public (in case of a publically-held corporation) and employees justification for the company's existence.

2.2   The corporate strategic plan begins with the mission statement. Management formulates short and long range goals from this statement. Descending goals are then developed for each major unit of the business.

2.3   The mission statement is a written description of the company leadership's vision and corporate direction *in terms easily understood by all employees*. The leaders' vision is the personal way the company plans to do business. Management and employee decisions are not to violate the mission statement (or the prime directive), the basic premise of *why you are in business.* The mission statement's purpose is to provide a company-wide bond and a single-minded approach to producing company profits.

3.0   Mission Statement Format

3.1   The mission statement is a short message of the company's relationship and expectations with respect to customers, employees, community, and the company. The most obvious is profit, but there may be other reasons for its existence, *provided the company is profitable.* Other purposes may be as an asset or provider of necessary services to the people in the community and an opportunity for employee's personal growth and development. Writing a brief description using action verbs in the sentence structure helps the owners and managers focus on company goals. For example, while remaining profitable is paramount, the business achieves profits by establishing and maintaining goals for such important elements as customer satisfaction, productivity, and quality. The mission statement ties all those factors together.

3.2   List critical attributes necessary to ingrain in employees such as those described in the preceding paragraph. The purpose is to set a common direction for everyone within the company.

3.3   List what the company provides its employees. This is a realistic and truthful statement of what it takes to achieve employee safety, well-being, and contentment.

3.4   The development of the mission statement begins with the completion of the attached form, A-100A. Prioritize the list of topics as:

A- Important, must be in the statement.

B- Some importance, could be in the statement.

C- Not very important, not necessary for the statement.

Next, explain what the topic means to you as manager.

3.5   Upon completion of form A-100A draft the mission statement using the "A" priorities and, space permitting, some of the "B" priorities. The entire mission statement may be three sentences or three paragraphs, *but confined to one page.* It must be easily understood and brief. If employees do not understand what it means, they will not respond as intended. If the mission statement is too long, employees lose sight of the big picture and get mired in the (unnecessary) details.

4.0   Conclusion

4.1   Review the corporate mission statement annually with employees, reminding them that it serves as a constant reminder as to the purpose of the company's existence. The vision for the company rarely changes; however, since the mission statement is the foundation from which company plans take root, the statement must be structurally sound.

4.2   Post the mission statement on large placards in conspicuous places as a reference for all employees and individual managers, becoming groundwork for decision-making and performance evaluations.

4.3   The owner is *keeper of the vision*. Other employees may be involved in the statement formulation, but the responsibility of the completed mission statement remains with the owner. In addition, the owner is responsible for maintaining adherence and awareness of the mission statement throughout the corporate structure.

FORM A-100A

<u>Topic</u> <u>Importance</u> <u>VISION - How Do You See The Company?</u>

Profit
Market Type
Market Niche
Sales Growth
Co. Growth
Customer Service
Competition
Creativity
Training
Quality
Technical
Safety
Ethics
Integrity
Vendors
Community
Country
Other

   This format is simply a representation of the items you will need to evaluate to establish the mission statement. Obviously you're going to need more than a few words to describe the item's importance and your vision. So take the space you need to do a thorough job, then condense your thoughts and write out the one page (maximum) mission statement.

TWELVE MANAGEMENT RULES TO LIVE BY

As a company organizes and staffs to achieve success, it typically operates within a framework of well-defined management principles. The difficulty lies not in gaining acceptance of those basic management concepts, but in implementing them when dealing with *specific individuals in actual situations.*

This operating procedure defines twelve rules which the owner of a trade contacting business and the employees who work for him can begin utilizing immediately when dealing with people issues.

1.0 The Rules

The 12 ground rules which follow will help you face and deal with tough people decisions.

1. Recognize that it is people, not structural changes, that make an organization work or fail. Organizational change alone is rarely the answer. *High-quality, talented employees who are dedicated can make almost any organizational structure succeed.* Conversely, lackluster employees who are poor performers will be ineffective under even the best organizational arrangement. Of course, organizational changes often are necessary to better utilize employee talents, achieve better planning and control, and reduce costs. But the manager must assure that he doesn't fall into the trap of tinkering with the organization as a means of escaping or putting off fundamental problems that are difficult or uncomfortable to deal with.

2. Provide for a successor. Every manager, other than individual contributors or professionals where a backup can't be economically justified, should have somebody in the organization that is potentially qualified for his job. If there is no one who has this potential, then you must give top priority to bringing someone in who does. (See *Succession Plan*).

3. Providing for a successor does not automatically mean adding to staff. Rather, it means that you should identify a few key promotable employees within the organization and groom them accordingly. If none of such employees exist, your job as owner is to replace those with employees who do have the talent and drive to succeed. Do this when attrition requires hiring replacements or when you're replacing marginal performers.

4. Deal with tenure problems fairly but candidly. Some individuals who have long and distinguished records of service in the company reach a point where their job responsibilities move beyond their energy level or capabilities. This is a natural development and should be expected. It happens eventually to all of us. The owner has an obligation to those employees who have served it loyally. You should compensate them fairly and give them assignments where they have an opportunity to make a continuing contribution. But, if they can no longer pull their own weight, you must remove them from the mainstream. It is not fair to the rest of the organization to leave them in positions they are no longer able to handle. And, it is certainly not fair to them. The manager must promptly inform those who cannot stand the pace so that they may make the necessary adjustments without delay.

5. Communicate expectations, then measure performance and act on results. A successful trade contractor assures that *each person in the organization knows what is expected of him, how his assignment fits into the whole operation, and how his performance will be measured.* Each individual should have a set of specified goals that he is expected to accomplish within a certain time frame, so that there will be no misunderstanding about what he is supposed to do. Actual accomplishment against those expected results should serve as the basic measure of performance. At the same time, the company's system of rewards and penalties must reinforce this concept. *Rewards should be for achieving results, not for effort.* In a competitive free enterprise environment, trying hard is not enough. *Achieving results is what counts—the difference between winning and losing.* Don't put up with marginal performers. The most frequent and insidious personal mistake owners are apt to make is to *live too long with marginal or poor performers.* Most kid themselves into thinking that by allowing these individuals to continue, they are being fair and that somehow time will correct the situation. Nothing could be further from the truth. Basic personality faults or skill deficiencies simply do not get corrected with time. It is totally unfair and a reflection of weak management to reach an agonizing conclusion that someone can't do the job after he has been on it for several years.

6. Criticize only in private. No person should be criticized in the presence of his subordinates. Any criticism should be saved for a private discussion so that the individual responsible can later handle the problem or correct matters with his subordinates on his own.

7. Weed out misfits. It is inevitable that some misfits are certain to creep into any organization, no matter how carefully people are screened or evaluated. The manager must be alert to move quickly and decisively to separate them. Not acting quickly detracts from a manager's credibility. Employees in an organization invariably know who the misfits are and will quickly draw negative conclusions about the manager's own capability if he permits them to remain.

8. Cultivate individual ambition and drive. No individual should be criticized simply because he is too ambitious, too aggressive, too impatient, or too demanding as long as he is a good thinker and fair and straightforward in his dealings and actions with others. These phrases frequently are used in a critical vein in performance evaluations, but they actually represent the kind of qualities an organization should develop, because such people can and will make things happen for the better. It is those people who are too easy going, too willing to compromise principles to avoid conflict, more interested in being liked than in getting things done, who should come under fire. They create a mushy working environment that makes it impossible to develop a strong team or achieve outstanding results.

9. Focus objectively on personal accomplishments, not personal differences. A manager must understand that race, age, sex, heritage, and socio-cultural characteristics have nothing whatsoever to do with evaluating an individual's effectiveness in a company. Focus on and evaluate the things that really count:

   ❖ Who faces problems squarely? Who has the guts to tell it like it is? Who does not?

   ❖ Who is an effective, contributing team member? Who is not?

   ❖ Who has and can articulate good ideas? Who cannot?

   ❖ Who produces results? Who meets his or her commitments? Who does not?

10. Let people know their status and prospects. The owner should assure that employees understand exactly where they stand and what their career outlook is at all times—even if it hurts. This doesn't mean that anyone should expect to have a special career path mapped out or promised a future promotion. But it does mean that *each person is entitled to know whether he is performing well or poorly in his current assignment and whether he is regarded as having future growth potential.*

11. Provide training, but stress self-development. There will be times when a company must reach outside to find the best available leadership to meet its management needs and standards. However, promotion from within should be the company's overall organizational plan and goal. Toward that end, a company should support projects to prepare its people for increased responsibilities. But, in the final analysis, all of us ultimately shape and control our individual destinies. A company can point the way and assist with company-sponsored educational and training programs, but self development is the key to success, and each of us must shoulder that responsibility on his own.

12. Create and maintain an attractive, healthy company environment. This last ground rule sums up all the previous guidelines. It underscores the essential responsibility of a manager to provide people in the organization with an opportunity to work effectively in a common effort, develop their capabilities, fulfill their professional aspirations, and achieve appropriate recognition and rewards. A manager must place major emphasis on creating this kind of environment. This doesn't mean he should seek to make everyone happy or to make tasks easier. But, it does mean that he should develop a work environment that has these characteristics:

   ❖ There is absolute honesty and integrity in what everyone says and does. And, everyone feels perfectly free to say what he or she really thinks.

   ❖ There is open communication up and down and across the organization. Everyone recognizes both the right and the responsibility to be open and constructively critical of things that are wrong or that could be improved.

   ❖ Owners should be willing to really listen to the other person's side and point of view, and willing to admit they're wrong if facts and logic show that is the case.

   ❖ There is a genuine interest in getting problems up on the table, and in correcting them rather than worrying about pinpointing blame or scurrying to keep shirt tails clean.

   ❖ Everyone works hard and effectively as a team, and has fun doing it. There is an air of excitement in the organization that comes with the realization that you are on a winning team. Unless this kind of environment exists, good people will leave and only mediocre people will remain. And, any company staffed with mediocrity is certain to lose.

PART FOUR

RUNNING A HIGH ENERGY AND PROFITABLE OPERATION

This section describes the heart of the trade contractor's business, and the place he is most likely to experience problems that create project setbacks. The following procedures describe specific jobs and practices the trade contactor will need to adopt to keep the operating part of his business profitable:

Site superintendent and project management

Bidding jobs

Daily field report

Corrective and preventive action plans

Implementing change orders

Inventory control

Quality and customer complaints

Purchasing

Loss control

SITE SUPERINTENDENT AND PROJECT MANAGEMENT

The primary purpose of this position guide is to establish and define the authority, accountability, reporting relationships, duties, responsibilities, and performance standards to successfully fulfill the position of site superintendent at ABC Enterprises, a trade contracting firm. The secondary purpose is to describe what successful project management means.

Perhaps more than any other position in the trade contracting company other than the owner, the site superintendent is responsible for overseeing the company's daily operations. It's important that we take a closer look at the site superintendent's responsibilities since his position is critical.

1.0   Job Description Summary

The site superintendent is responsible for the day to day leadership of all assigned field projects. He could be the field superintendent for a large construction project, the working manager of the laborers installing your gutters, or any other person who manages the actual trade contracting work. (For a list of trade contractors and subcontractors, see *Appendix: (2) Examples of Types of Trade Contractors and Subcontractors.*) He is responsible for directing the efforts of the crew(s) and subcontractors to meet or do better than job estimates for both labor and material. The superintendent communicates daily with site employees to review the day's work requirements. The superintendent inspects all assigned projects to assure the project meets quality standards and customer commitments.

2.0   Reporting Relationship

❖ The superintendent reports directly to the company owner in smaller organizations and to a vice president in a larger operation.

❖ Reporting to the superintendent are the assigned crews performing the actual trade contracting work. In larger operations many field supervisors may report to the site superintendent.

3.0   Skill, Knowledge and Abilities

❖ Personal Skills: Uses analytical and observational skills to organize, forecast, and control workflow and all project functions.

❖ Physical: Works both inside and outside. Body positions include standing, stooping, bending, kneeling, sitting, and walking.

Corrected vision is essential. Must be able to walk and negotiate physical barriers such as rooftops and contracting equipment, climb up and down ladders, and around company facilities and customer locations.

- ❖ Body movements: Carrying items up to seventy-five (75) pounds, use of hands, eyes, arms and voice.
- ❖ Mental: A blend of analytical and mathematical skills is required. Must be able to read, write, and communicate clearly person to person and on the telephone. Multi-language skills a plus.

4.0   Working Conditions

- ❖ A large percentage of work is in a non-climate controlled job-site environment.
- ❖ Exposed to hazards of construction sites and moving and dangerous equipment.
- ❖ Individual schedules depend upon the project. Some overtime may be required. The work is fast-paced and may be stressful with actions expected to yield results.

5.0   Authority

- ❖ The superintendent is given the authority to direct supervisors and crews to meet the productivity and quality goals established. The superintendent is responsible for the resolution of any employee disciplinary issues or actions.

6.0   Duties and Responsibilities

- ❖ Plan and organize work so that all crews are working effectively. Control on-site hours in accordance with the project schedule to control costs and achieve completion dates.
- ❖ Assure that employees follow all safety procedures.
- ❖ Respond to customer and external requests in a polite and professional manner. Use commonsense resolution where possible, and if he encounters a problem he is unable to handle he should ask the company owner for assistance.
- ❖ Approve all site time cards and subcontractor completion work.
- ❖ Help all crew leaders and employees in the interpretation of plans or specifications to assure quality workmanship.

7.0   Project Management

- ❖ Responsible for familiarization with the complete scope and proposed method of contracting for all assigned projects.

❖ Review and become familiar with all job drawings, specifications, and schedules provided for the project by the company owner.

❖ If extra work is being done on a time and material basis, the superintendent will complete the daily log as required. Each log includes man-hours worked, materials consumed or delivered to job site, and special tools and equipment used in the work. The superintendent is to have the owner or owner's representative sign this log at the end of each day. (See also *Daily Work Progress Report*).

❖ Personally oversee and accept accountability for all actions taken or not taken on the job-site.

❖ Develop and communicate job scope, estimated hours, and time schedules to supervisors and crew members. Work with the crews installing parts and materials and keep them supplied so their progress is uninterrupted.

❖ Identify and advise the company owner of requests for work (potential change orders) that are outside the scope of the contract.

❖ Assures that job sites are continually cleaned up, materials properly stored, and equipment maintained and operated properly.

❖ At the end of the day, assures that the job site is secure:
  o Any required barricades are in place.
  o All tools are locked up.
  o Office and storage trailers are locked.
  o Owner's premises are locked, if appropriate.
  o All debris properly cleaned up.
  o Equipment properly shut down, stored and plugged in as required.
  o Job site is safe.

❖ On a weekly basis, reviews tool and equipment inventory lists assigned to the project. Verify, corrects, and relays the pertinent information to the appropriate owner or other assigned employee responsible for reviewing it.

❖ Workflow
  o Co-ordinate the daily work schedules for all employees and subcontractors.
  o Meet or improve budgeted hours and project completion deadlines.
  o Maintain proper staffing to complete project on time while controlling costs.

- o Consult with supervisors and crews regarding tasks of a critical nature to avoid scrap and rework and customer complaints.
  - o Request, at least one day in advance, all necessary additional tools and equipment and promptly tag and report all broken or non-functioning tools and equipment.
- ❖ Purchasing, receiving and inventory control
  - o When shortages occur, requisition parts and materials from the owner in advance so that the workflow is not disrupted.
  - o Assure that parts and materials received at the job site are in accordance with the bill of lading. If discrepancies occur, note on the bill of lading before signing and notify the company owner as soon as possible. Return bills of lading to the owner each week.
  - o Assure physical inventory control procedures are in place and used to protect the materials, equipment, and supplies at the job site.
  - o Assure all surplus materials and equipment are promptly returned to the warehouse or transferred to another project.
- ❖ Timecards
  - o As part of the daily log, submit time cards to accounting (in a small business the person responsible for administrative tasks) for each crew member with hours assigned to the proper cost code.
- ❖ Reports, communications, and meetings
  - o Maintain open channels of communications with the company owner.
  - o Assure that required field reports are completed and are submitted on time.
  - o Estimate percent of completion on-site for each phase of the project.
  - o Establish and maintain necessary job files at the job site.
  - o Attend job meetings as requested by the owner.
  - o As required or requested, conduct end day telephone conferences with the owner to assess progress, redirect efforts, solve problems, and take corrective actions.
- ❖ Quality
  - o Assure that all work performed meets contract and company quality standards.

- o In conjunction with the owner, schedule inspections as appropriate.
- o Monitor the work performed by all subcontractors.
- o Meet with subcontractors as required to provide secure information and resolve problems.
- o Identify quality problems in the work performed by subcontractors and direct them to correct problems.
- o Recommend to the owner the removal of any subcontractor who is not performing effectively and to company quality standards.

❖ Safety
- o Assure compliance with all safety and regulatory agency requirements.
- o Enforce a dress code for all employees and subcontractors that conforms to OSHA standards.
- o Perform safety inspections at the job site and implement corrective actions as required.

❖ Employees
- o Lead by example, providing public praise and private constructive criticism.
- o Hold the assigned crews accountable for the results of their actions, taken or not taken.
- o As directed, conduct performance evaluations for all direct report positions.
- o Perform other related duties as requested by the company owner. As authorized, assist or function on behalf of the owner on a project.
- o Maintain harmonious relations with everyone associated with the project.

❖ Equipment
- o Assure that all material, equipment and tools are stored properly.
- o Assure that leased equipment is functioning and within specifications to perform the work prior to accepting the equipment.
- o Solicit added work from customers based on need and benefit of the work.
- o As required, perform the duties of a crew leader or crew member.

❖ Judgment and Decision Making
- o Demonstrates good judgment and reasoning when investigating and solving problems.

- o Respects the confidentially of customer, company, and employee information.
- ❖ Relationships with others
  - o Acts as an example, treating all contacts with respect.
  - o Demonstrates ability to accept constructive criticism without resentment, instituting change where appropriate.
  - o Creates positive solutions to difficult situations, maintaining personal confidence and self-esteem.
  - o Handles difficult situations tactfully, fostering and maintaining personal confidence and self-esteem at all levels.
- ❖ Initiative
  - o Personally strives for self-improvement. Fosters it with direct report employees.
  - o Immediately notifies the owner of current or impending issues that may impact the company. Offers constructive suggestions on these issues.
- ❖ Attendance and Reliability
  - o Exemplary attendance standards are expected.

8.0   Measurements of Performance

- ❖ Assigned construction projects are completed according to time schedules and within material and man-hour requirements.
- ❖ No work is performed beyond the scope of signed contracts without approval from the owner.
- ❖ All contracting work (including subcontractor's work) meets contract specifications and company quality standards, and warranty work is less than the maximum allowable by company policy.
- ❖ Maintains a safe work site with no lost time accidents. Enforces and documents established safety and regulatory guidelines.
- ❖ Completes and submits timecards accurately and on time.
- ❖ Minimizes tool loss and equipment failures resulting from improper operation.
- ❖ Maintains effective communication between the job site and the office.
- ❖ Demonstrates good judgment, reporting on key issues or opportunities to the owner.
- ❖ Works in an independent and expeditious manner with minimal supervision.
- ❖ Coordinates efforts between contractor and subcontractors.

- ❖ As directed, evaluates performance of all full-time subordinates on time and provides a means for them to meet or exceed standards.
- ❖ Respects the confidentiality of company, customer, and employee information, encouraging subordinates to do the same.
- ❖ Satisfactorily performs all other duties, as requested, by the owner.

BIDDING JOBS

The process of bidding for new business and tracking what happens to those bids are functions which determine the success of small companies such as trade contractors. The attention to detail and accuracy in bid preparation and tracking is often the deciding factor in the growth and effective operation of a trade contracting business. (See also *Estimating and Tracking.*)

1.0   The Heart of the Trade Contractor's Business
1.1 The process of bidding for new business and tracking what happens to those bids determine the success of the contracting business. The attention to detail and accuracy in bid preparation and tracking is often the deciding factor in the company's growth and effective operation.

1.2 The preparation and organization of work papers, estimates, and forms in a systematic way is necessary for consistent performance in bidding practices and follow up required to track the success of the bids.

1.3 The purpose of this standard procedure is to explain the method of attaining clearly specified cost estimates, bids, and tracking reports.

2.0   Preparing Bids
2.1 A standard bid form should include a heading for customer identification and job site data along with the contracting company's internal job number identification.

2.2 Enter the total of all parts and material cost from the bill of materials.

2.3 Include labor estimates.

2.4 Summarize other direct costs on this form as follows:

2.4.1 Subcontracting. This section is the place to enter bid prices or estimates for subcontracted work. The estimator must strive to make sure that the subcontract bid includes all possible costs.

2.4.2 Equipment rental. Include equipment rental cost for an accurate job bid. The estimator must be certain that fees for delivery, maintenance, accessories, late charges, and taxes are included in this item.

2.4.3 Other. Other direct costs include license fees, performance bonds, insurance premiums, permits and other incidentals. This item can also be used to recover the cost of small consumable supplies used on the job. Again, careful planning is required to assure coverage of all costs.

3.0   Job Summary

3.1 Completion of the job summary section of the bid form requires the addition of materials, labor and other direct costs to arrive at total direct costs.

3.2 Calculate labor burden and enter the dollar value.

3.3 Calculate overhead allocation for the job and enter the dollar value.

3.4 Add total direct costs, burden, and overhead to arrive at total job cost. This can be looked at as the breakeven for this job. Bids should not be made below this cost *unless the owner approves otherwise.*

3.5 Profit. The final step of bid preparation is the determination of the profit desired from the job. To arrive at the final bid price divide the total job cost by the result of subtracting the desired profit from 100%. For example if the desired profit is 20 percent and the total job cost is $500 calculate the profit as follows:

$500 / (100 % - 20%) = 500 / 0.80 = $625

Profit $ = $625 - $500 = $125

Proof: $125 / $625 = 0.20

3.6 The selling price of the job is then the total of total job cost and profit. This may or may not be the price quoted on the final bid.

4.0   Quoting Prices

4.1 The final bid quote is a result of three factors:

4.1.1 What the trade contractor *must* have to cover his costs.

4.1.2 What the competition has or will bid.

4.1.3 How badly the company wants or needs the job either from a particular customer (a gateway to future business) or the cash flow from this particular project.

4.2 At this point you can see that sound estimating practices are essential so that the owner of the company has confidence in the ability to maneuver from the job breakeven point. Successful quoting is a skill that is learned and can be improved with over time with experience.

5.0   Job Tracking

5.1 Once bids are completed you then compare actual job cost and profit to the estimate. Not to do so is a serious lapse in project management. The value of this information in making management decisions is immense.

5.2 Compare bids to completed job data using the information that follows:

5.2.1   Actual total job cost.

5.2.2   Actual material cost.

5.2.3   Actual labor cost.

5.2.4   Actual phase costs.

5.2.5   Competitive bids.

5.2.6   Actual profit (dollars and percent).

5.2.7   Actual subcontract costs.

5.2.8   Actual equipment rental costs.

5.2.9   Actual other costs.

5.2.10   Actual completion dates.

5.3 With this information available, company owners will be able to identify those areas where bidding is off target. The reasons for the deficit can then be identified and corrected.

THE JOB PLAN

Planning and goal setting are essential parts of every job. A plan of action must be established with definitive goals and objectives so that work effort and resources are directed in a controlled and coordinated manner toward their accomplishment.

A good job plan establishes goals and objectives your company needs to reach for every one of its jobs, whether you're fitting sealed weatherproof windows to a home or installing the plumbing for a large commercial building (or any other trade contacting application). The course of action is a means of direction that shows how to reach the objective.

Effective managers direct their employees. They manage their jobs every day without losing sight of the goals and objectives. They make decisions and changes as required to keep the job progressing toward achieving goals.

Without a job plan, a job will tend to run on historical experience or in a crisis management mode. Employees work in different directions due to lack of common goals. This creates confusion, inefficiency and, in effect, excessive cost and lower profits.

The lack of a job plan limits management effectiveness. Efforts are based on day-to-day situations resulting in a loss of focus on the long term (relative to the job) goals and objectives. Essentially, the trade contractor is flying blind. Although managers cannot plan for all contingencies, planning will reduce risk and provide guidelines for staying on course.

Actually, trade contractors make job plans every day . . . in their heads. But like any other task with a great deal of variables, the mind often forgets details. So it is imperative that trade contractors shift their focus and write out job plans.

1.0 The Job Plan

A job plan should be produced as a part of the bidding process that is prior to bidding or accepting a job. This is because all the elements of a job plan should be part of the information necessary to develop a good proposal.

Start with a job statement: A job statement sums up the work in a short, narrowly constructed sentence. It describes the finished product and service and should be considered a guide.

The next step is to identify the job goals. These are generally, defined by the customer in the bidding process.

Once the job goals are established, a more defined course of action must be set for job completion. This course of action is determined by the job objectives. Job objectives fall into two categories; completion objectives and management or corporate objectives.

❖ Completion objectives are those interim objectives that identify the actions and results required by the client at job completion.
They also may be defined by the customer in his request for bid or other related documents. If the customer doesn't specify them, the job manager should establish them as a set of guidelines for job progress determination. They may be obtained by answering these questions:
  a) What is the time schedule for the job?
  b) What is the deliverable schedule for the job?
  c) What resources do we need?
  d) When do we need these resources?
  e) What are the reasonable divisions of the job or
  f) What is the definition of job completion?
❖ Management or corporate objectives are those objectives that identify the actions and results required by the trade contractor at job completion. These objectives are obtained by answering the questions:
  a) What profit levels do we reasonably expect?
  b) Can this job be billed in progress payments?
  c) What are the reasonable divisions of the job or
  d) What resources do we need?
  e) When do we need those resources?
  f) What is the definition of job completion?

Please note that many of the questions listed above are identical, just arranged differently. That is because the information needed is generally the same; however, the emphasis is different based on the differing requirements of the customer and the trade contractor.

2.0 Job Budget

Once you establish the job goals and objectives, prepare a job budget. This budget shall consist of a listing of the resources to be applied to the job and their approximate scheduling. Additionally, the budget shall contain the cost of those resources (e.g., billing rates times hours for the employees involved, mileage charge plus markup, and cost plus markup for materials and supplies).

Since the job budget is for a relatively short period of time, it must be detailed so that actual performance can be measured against plan and corrective action taken where necessary.

3.0 Use of the Job Plan

The job plan should be used:

❖ In the bidding process as:

a)   An aid to creation of the bid package.

b)   A way to collect and present assumptions made in creation of the bid package.

c)   A way of showing the customer that the trade contractor is qualified for and understands the job.

d)   A schedule for deliverables for the customer.

e)   A justification for requesting progress payments from the customer based on the schedule of deliverables in

f)   A method of putting boundaries around the job.

❖ In the work effort as:

a)   An identification of the assumptions made in defining the job.

b)   A means of assuring that resources estimated for the job are measured against actual resources and corrective action

c)   A schedule for delivery to the customer.

d)   A justification for requesting progress payments from the customer based on the schedule of deliverables in the job plan.

e)   A means of identifying that the boundaries around the job have been breached and there has been a change in job

f)   A positive indication of job completion.

❖ In the billing process as:

a)   An identification of the assumptions made in defining the job.

b)   A justification for requesting progress payments from the customer based on the schedule of deliverables in the job plan.

c)   A means of identifying that the boundaries around the job have been breached and the there has been a change in job

d)   Positive indication of job completion.

4.0 Forms

The job planning sheet (Form H-100-A shown below) is a form used for creating a job plan once you establish goals. This form should be filled in by the individual responsible on the trade contractor's team for the job. Once complete, it is returned to a manager or supervisor who reviews it with the project coordinator (in a small company these jobs may well be held by one employee) and approves the plan. A copy of the form is then returned to the project coordinator who now moves forward to achieve the goal. The manager or supervisor periodically checks to determine progress.

5.0 Summary

The procedure described above is a guideline for constructing goals and objectives into a job plan. A good job plan may take several hours to complete.

Planning and setting goals is the first function of a manager. Whether documented or not, there is be a purpose to be accomplished by the job. To facilitate communication, it is desirable that the purpose be specified in writing. The company's prime objective in accepting any job is to make a profit. The success and future of the company ultimately depends on its ability to complete jobs efficiently, effectively, and in a profitable manner.

Form H-100-A
Job Planning Sheet
(As seen on this page and the next two pages)

Customer_____

Address_____

Job # _____   Date   _____

Job Description_____

_____

List   of   equipment   and   facilities   that   will   be
required:_____

_____

Anticipated labor requirements:

	Number	Estimated Labor Cost
Employees:	_____	$ _____
Supervisors:	_____	$ _____
Managers:	_____	$ _____

Anticipated equipment costs:

	Existing Equipment	Equipment Costs
Items:	_____	$ _____
	_____	$ _____
	_____	$ _____
	_____	$ _____

New equipment capital expenditures:

Item		
	_____	$ _____
	_____	$ _____
Total job cost (estimated)		$ _____

Difficulties anticipated (if any):

_____

Deliverables required and scheduled:

_____

_____

Job is Complete when (list completion requirements):

_____

_____

_____

Job Bid Price: $ _____

Bid Price Based on: T&M ___   Fixed Price ___ Cost + Fixed Fee ___

Other (describe) _____

Anticipated profit: percentage: _____ $ _____

Prepared by: Name: _____   Date: _____

DAILY WORK PROGRESS REPORT

The daily work progress report is the way that the owner and filed communicate. Without it job progress may falter. Daily information from the job site keeps the trade contractor on top of his most important jobs.

The following procedure outlines the responsibilities and methods used to complete a daily work progress report.

1.0 Responsibility

The lead man or job supervisor on each and every contracting job is responsible for completing a daily work progress report. The completed reports are turned in to the office either every day or on each Friday along with employee time sheets. The company owner reviews competed job reports to assure progress to the job plan, then files them in the appropriate job folders.

Please note that for smaller trade contractors a daily verbal report may suffice, depending on how the company owner wants to handle it. The important thing is to make sure that the company is not falling behind schedule for promised customer completion dates.

2.0 Information

At the beginning of each job the owner briefs the field manager and provides the following information:

❖ The number of labor hours scheduled for the job.
❖ A copy of the bill of materials for the job.
❖ A review of the job plan, specifically how progress is expected.
❖ A list of any subcontract work or rental equipment needed for the job.

3.0 **Filling in the Daily Work Progress Report** (See example at end of this section)

The supervisor or lead person fills in the following information:

❖ HEADER INFORMATION. Fill in the day and date and the name or number of the job he is working on.
❖ EMPLOYEES WORKING. List of the names of the men and women assigned to the job and *actually* working for that specific day, including the hours each worked during the day and the number of *paid* hours the men report on their time sheets (needless to say, those numbers must match).

- ❖ TOTAL HOURS. The supervisor or lead man totals up the number of employee-hours, including his own for the day.
- ❖ TOTAL JOB HOURS. This is a running total of *all* hours worked on this job. For example:
  - o 1st day of job – 16 hours
  - o 2nd day of job – 24 hours
  - o Total job hours - 40 hours.
- ❖ HOURS BID. This is the number of labor hours in the bid.
- ❖ PERCENT HOURS USED. Divide the total hours used to date on the job by the hours bid. The result is the percent of the bid hours used on the job.
- ❖ WORK ACCOMPLISHED TODAY. In a simple statement, describe the work that the crew accomplished for the specific day.
- ❖ PERCENT COMPLETE. Estimate the amount of work which is actually completed on the job.
- ❖ WEATHER CONDITION. A simple statement of weather conditions which may affect job progress.
- ❖ PLANS FOR TOMORROW. What phase of the work is planned for tomorrow? Is there an alternate plan if weather conditions change?
- ❖ CHANGE ORDERS AND PROBLEMS. Problems which need to be addressed by the company owner. Is the customer asking for a change in the original scope of work? Are there rental equipment or tool needs that need to be taken care of to make sure that the job stays on schedule? Are there problems with subcontract work?

DAILY WORK PROGRESS REPORT

Job: Henderson Elevator Cab Installation   **Field Supervisor:** Sam Jones

Date: August 25, 2012

Employee	Hours Worked Today	Hours Worked Cumulative	Total Job Hours Worked
Mike Smith	8	8	
Pete Jones	8	8	16
Ralph Burns	8	8	24
Ron Murphy	8	8	32

Total Job Bid Hours	Total Job Hours Worked To Date	Percent Completion
350	175	50

Weather conditions today: Working indoors

Plans for tomorrow: Continue installation

Change orders/Problems: None today

CORRECTIVE AND PREVENTIVE ACTION PLANS

Action plans—or any other plans for that matter—are insufficient if a mechanism isn't in place to take corrective actions when you find problems, as well as preventive action for future occurrences of the same problems. The purpose of the procedure described below is to outline a method for taking corrective action as needed, monitoring the effectiveness of the action, and implementing preventive action to reduce the possibility of the problem occurring again. Nothing is more frustrating to employees than watching the same problem repeat itself over and over. It's also a morale killer. And it destroys employees' faith in company owners and managers.

We live in an imperfect world. There will always be things that go wrong. You must try to limit those things because they cost money. Each of us makes mistakes, even our employees. It is not shameful to make mistakes. It is, however, shameful not to learn from those mistakes. And it is shameful to repeat them.

The purpose of corrective action is to take care of an immediate problem. The purpose of preventive action is to take steps to prevent a repeat performance. Corrective action makes the problem go away. Preventive action keeps it from coming back.

1.0 Corrective and Preventive Actions

Experienced managers should be able to institute corrective action on an individual basis (taking care of the customer's immediate problem). The corrective action normally affects most of the trade contractor's functions. For example, if a contractor's employees paint a house the wrong color, customers are unhappy and the cost of repainting lowers the company's profits. Employees needed for paying work find themselves repairing defective work, and the owner possibly fires a supervisor or lead employee.

Preventive action in this example might involve a check off sheet that matches paint color chips supplied by the customer with paint samples before staring painting. Simple preventive actions are always best but sometimes more complex solutions are required.

Fixing problems requires a team approach. Inexperienced managers especially should use the team approach for corrective action as well as preventive action until they have learned from the group and are comfortable deciding actions on their own.

Resolution of the immediate problem (corrective action), as well as the preventive action to avoid the problem in the future, must be thought through before taking action.

If the problem was caused by employee error, take the time to calm yourself before making any decisions or taking any disciplinary action.

On a sheet of paper write down the following headings, or use the attached form. Record the date, preventive and corrective actions, and employees responsible for those actions.

Corrective and Preventive Action Worksheet

Problem	Corrective Action	Preventive Action	Person Responsible for Action(s)	Completion Date

2.0 Problem Solving

The first step is to identify the problem or problems. What happened? Examine the problem in detail. In the process you may uncover other problems. Make note of them and refer back to those problems as separate issues. Do not mix more than one problem and do not get off the problem at hand.

Through the process of detailing what happened, you should be able to uncover the *root cause*. This is what caused the problem that you now must address, through actions that cure or stop it. You will need to address peripheral causes. However, if you do not find the root cause of the problem, you can address all of the peripheral causes and still not solve the main problem.

Once you feel confident that you have identified all of the peripheral causes and the root cause, address each cause with the corrective action that you feel will solve the problem and the preventive action to keep it from recurring. Often the corrective action and the preventive action are the same, but many times they are different. For example, in the wrong color paint problem, the corrective action is to repaint the house; the preventive action is to have two employees double-check the specified paint on the job order (match color chips) with the customer's bill of materials *before* painting begins.

The key to corrective and preventive action is the *action itself.* Identify the person responsible for taking the action and the time frame for implementing the correction and preventive measures. Document the information on the Corrective and Preventive Action Worksheet (shown above) and then *take action.*

As I mentioned before, and this always bears repeating *it is not enough to resolve the current problem. You must also analyze what needed steps to prevent the same problem from happening again.* Document this action with assigned responsibility and a time frame for completion.

Corrective and preventive action is how we show our intelligence. We accept mistakes but we learn from them and do not accept them a second time.

3.0 Follow Up

You have just solved a problem and initiated preventive action to keep the problem from recurring. Or have you? The next step is a follow up to see if you were right and the action solved the problem and prevented it from recurring. Did it work as you thought it would? Did it cause other problems as you solved this one? You follow up to assure that the action has met your expectations. If not, you must go through the process again and find a solution that does. You repeat the process until you are satisfied with the results.

4.0 Summary

When problems occur, use this procedure. Investigate and keep investigating until the whole story comes out. Owners and managers should not make snap judgments or take action until they have followed the process.

As with the other employees, management can make mistakes. By following up on corrective and preventive actions, management will see their mistakes and select new courses of action. The end result is that you accomplish the mission.

IMPLEMENTING CHANGE ORDERS

Change orders are an organized way to make changes to established and agreed-upon specifications and bills of material between the trade contractor and his customer. Anytime a customer requests changes after-the-fact, or anytime a trade contractor makes changes to increase profits, reduce costs, or improve quality, there's a price.

As a trade contractor, you should *always* ask extra for changes requested by the customer. And anytime you make changes you need to get approval of the customer or face his wrath when he finds out. For example, if you substitute a plastic molding in place of a wood molding because the plastic is cheaper, it's your duty to make sure the customer signs off on it *before* you make the change.

Regardless of who initiates the change order, record the changes in writing on a change order log, specify the cost differential and its effect on the total price, and you and the customer both sign-off to indicate agreement. This prevents any misunderstandings or disputes several weeks or months later when memories fade. Be sure to describe the change itself, and any charges for additional labor and materials. An example of a change order log follows:

Change Order Log

Construction Company
Address
City, State, ZIP
Phone Number

Date: _____
Owner: _____
Contract amount: _____
Project name: _____
Project number: _____

S = Submitted A = Approved R = Rejected

C.O. number	Description	Amount	Schedule change	Status		
				S	A	R

Page _____ of _____

INVENTORY CONTROL

Without effective inventory control a trade contractor can find himself out of business before he knows it. Excess money tied up in unusable or excess inventory destroys profits and it does so quickly. *This point, more than most others, separates successful trade contractors from those who fail.*

1.0 Minimize and Control Inventory
The purpose of this standard procedure is to define and explain the controls and systems required to maintain an inventory control system for ABC Trade Contractors utilized for minimizing, ordering, and controlling parts and materials.

2.0 Procedure
2.1 The inventory for a trade contractor should be classified into the following groupings:
   ❖ Materials.
   ❖ Tooling.

2.2 In order to establish and maintain an accurate inventory control system, once the system has been set up, take a physical inventory of all the items to be maintained in controlled inventory. This information should contain quantity, in units, item name, part number, description, and unit cost.

2.3 All items set up in the controlled inventory system (computerized or manual) must be designated by name, number, and the unit of measure.

2.4 Once these inventory controls have been established, all transactions occurring after the physical inventory date are to be recorded and the information provided to the owner or manager who will then be aware of the updated inventory status. (Today, more than ever, inventory is managed by basic inventory control software, although a manual system is sufficient for a smaller trade contractor.)
   ❖ For example, receipts of items purchased should be recorded from the invoice. All items received should be checked in physically to assure that the receipts match the order. Further, the receiving reports should be matched with the invoice prior to payment to insure correct billing and payment.

2.5 Under this procedure the controlled inventory (whether kept manually or on your computer system) will always indicate what is available for use as well as what has been used. Compare actual usage with sales to determine proper levels of usage (maintaining levels of inventory commensurate with job needs; none less, none more). Therefore, whenever the inventory of an item falls to a level deemed necessary to reorder, these items will be so indicated in your computer file (or manual inventory) as items needing to be reordered.

3.0 Reorder Points

3.1 Reorder points are established so that existing inventory will be sufficient to cover projected usage until new units ordered are received. This inventory point is arrived at by analysis of historical data of the inventory turns of each part.

If there is no monthly or weekly sales history, the weekly rate can be approximated by dividing the annual sales by 52. The formula then for reorder point is: *Lead time (in weeks) times weekly sales.*
For example: If lead time for a particular item is four weeks and annual usage is 24 units then the reorder point is $24/52 \times 4 = 2$ units. When two units remain on the shelf, then it is time to reorder.

3.2 The reorder point estimates the number of units that will be sold, at average or normal sales levels, while awaiting arrival of the next shipment.

3.3 The reorder point is the minimum quantity that should be kept on hand to achieve desired sales levels. Reorder points must be set up for each item in your controlled inventory.

4.0 Lead Time

4.1 Lead time from your vendors may be inconsistent. Lead times can vary from two suppliers for the same item, for example.

4.2 Keep a margin of safety stock to protect your operations. Responsible managers of the trade contracting company should analyze and determine specific material requirements. The plan must include a safety stock level that covers delays in shipments of frequently used parts and materials. The safety stock is decided on an individual item by item basis. This means that the consequences of an out of stock situation should be evaluated on an item by item basis.

5.0 Reorder Quantity

5.1 ABC Trade Contractor's current inventory coverage starts with available inventory records.

5.2 The basic guideline should be to determine the number of units for each item carried in inventory. Then maintain inventory stock levels at a maximum of "X" number of days' supply of these items. I say "X" because each trade contractor must determine the margin of safety stock for *every* part and material type carried in inventory.

5.3 However, monitor usage levels carefully because of changing needs based on the number of jobs on the books. Therefore, review all inventory requirements at least every three months.

5.4 In order to be in a position to accurately place an order for inventory resupply, prepare a stock status report that lists items and quantities on hand as of the date of the report. This can simply be the ending quantity on your most recent physical inventory.

5.5 Once all of the necessary information is available, placing restocking orders becomes routine.

6.0 Classification of Items

There are three general classifications of items carried in inventory.

6.1 The first level, "A" items, are those items where usage is in the top 20 percent by volume. These are ideal items for a min/max inventory control system since they will only need to be monitored for increases or decreases in usage. Once the levels are set, annual usage for these items will determine whether or not you need to adjust the min/max quantities. These items should always be in stock in ample quantities to support customer demand.

6.2 The second tier, "B" items, are those items that turn less than the desired 10 turns per year. These warrant little management attention aside from setting a minimum and maximum quantity. Maintain ABC Trade Contractor's "B" items at a level equal to the minimum order quantity allowed by the vendor. These are the next 20 percent of items in volume. When the stock of these items reaches a prescribed low level, then the next minimum order should be placed. Here, again, the trade contractor will have to determine what that low level is.

6.3 The third inventory level, or "C" items, are those 60 percent of inventory that account for roughly the bottom 10 percent of usage. These items should be weighed carefully to determine the benefit of maintaining a prescribed minimum in stock versus the risk of maintaining the inventory without reorder points. These are parts such as nuts and bolts commercially available from a local hardware store. It doesn't pay to spend time determining reorder points with items such as those.

6.4 . For most trade contractors, the focus on inventory control will be the "A" and "B" items.

7.0 Procedure for Establishing Min/Max Quantities

7.1 Obtain a usage report for the past 12 months for all items carried in inventory.

7.2 On an item by item basis determine the following:

❖ Seasonality. Does usage change with the time of year?

❖ Can you forecast possible problems or shortages from suppliers?

7.3 The minimum reorder point is the stock level that will support projected usage during the required lead time. This is the amount that will be used and sold while waiting for the next order to arrive. Examples are bricks for building a home, and replacement window sashes for older homes.

7.4 The maximum equals the minimum inventory level plus the reorder quantity. This is the maximum quantity that you should have in stock that should be able to support usage for no more than a 30 day period.

8.0   Open-to-Buy

The open-to-buy system (OTB) achieves targeted inventory costs through the reduction of inventory carrying costs. *This is a fairly complex system that is best handled by the company's accountant with the company owner or his designated representative, somebody who is good at numbers. Look at the OTB system as an additional tool that helps control the dollar amount of inventory.*

8.1 Objectives of the Open-to-Buy System

❖ The purchasing open-to-buy system establishes the dollar limit to which the designated manager is authorized to spend for parts and materials during a specific period of time, usually, one month.

❖ Therefore, the open-to-buy system becomes an instrument for controlling inventory dollars.

9.0   Required Data for OTB

All required information, except for the cost of open orders, is readily available from the company's balance sheet. The balance sheet is obtained from the company's accountant.

9.1 Determine the planning period and related subdivisions, i.e., one year broken into months or possibly a six month rolling average. The period for most trade contractors is one month.

9.2 Determine material categories; either all materials combined or specific categories. For the typical trade contractor one category of inventory will be controlled and that category is a combination of parts and materials.

9.3 Determine the (actual or estimated) beginning inventory and projected ending inventory values at cost.

9.4 Determine planned sales and cost of sales by the product categories. Historical data, budgets and forecasts, or a combination of these three can be used to make this determination.

9.5 Since inventories are valued at cost, it is necessary to determine the following amounts at cost for the planned period.

(1)   Beginning inventory value (actual or estimated).

(2)   Ending inventory (estimated).

(3)   Cost of sales for the planned period (for example, lumber used – dollar amount).

(4)   Value of inventory on order (outstanding purchase orders at the   beginning of the planned period).

9.6 Calculate inventory turnover rate as part of the ending inventory forecasting process. The inventory turnover rate should be based on the time required to receive delivery after placing an order with a vendor.

The formula for calculating the inventory turnover rate is as follows:

For inventory valued at cost:

$$\text{Turnover rate} = \frac{\text{Cost of sales for planned period}}{\text{Average inventory for the planned period}}$$

9.7 The formula to calculate average inventory for the planned period is as follows:

Based on the beginning and ending inventories:

$$\text{Average Inventory} = \frac{\text{Beginning inventory} + \text{Ending inventory}}{2}$$

Based on the projected month-end balances for the planned period (assume you have projected monthly inventory balances for the period of a year beginning with the last month of the previous year plus 12 months of the current year). Then:

$$\text{Average Inventory} = \frac{\text{The sum of the month end balances}}{13}$$

10.0   Open-to-Buy Procedures

10.1 The following formulas should be calculated for each

inventory category. For the average trade contractor, this will be done for a combination of parts and material types only.

❖ Use this formula for inventories valued at cost:

Purchasing limit = cost of sales - beginning inventory + ending inventory - parts and materials currently on order.

❖ The ending inventory should be the targeted inventory value set by the owners.

10.2 Example

Use of the open-to-buy system will provide a measure of control in reducing and maintaining inventories at profitable levels by reducing the amount of working capital dedicated to inventory and reducing inventory carrying costs.

The following schedule depicts the effects on the open-to-buy (OTB) purchasing limit calculations based on changes of the plan:

CHANGES TO PLAN   **EFFECT ON OTB LIMITS**
------------------------------   ------------------------------------

Sales above plan   Increase in limits
Sales below plan   decrease in limits
Purchases above plan   decrease in limits
Purchases below plan   increase in limits

Product Category	Cost of sales +	Beginning Inventory -	Ending Inventory +	Parts/materials on order -	OTB purchase limit =
A	100,000	30,000	25,000	3000	92,000

Proof
Beginning inventory   +30,000
Mdse on Order   + 3,000
OTB limit   +92,000
Cost of sale   - (100,000)
Ending inventory   25,000

11.0   Summary

11.1 The concept of minimum and maximum reorder points is designed to provide a simplified method of controlling the inventory levels. It requires the attention and assumes the specialized product knowledge of the manager responsible for administering the system.

11.2 The purpose is to make reordering quicker and easier, as well as more accurate.

11.3 The use of min/max inventory levels and reorder points and quantities are one component of a total inventory management system that will help the trade contractor control inventory costs and reduce the dollars tied up in inventory, while assuring that supplies are sufficient to meet demand throughout the year.

11.4 The open-to-buy system for controlling the dollar value of purchases is a tool for controlling the working capital tied up in inventory dollars. It is a system that allows the owners control at a glance without personally performing the purchasing function. By setting dollar limits and targets, ownership has quantifiable performance measures for the designated employees.

QUALITY AND CUSTOMER COMPLAINTS

There are three things certain in life: death, taxes, and if you're a trade contractor, customer complaints. Since the trade contractor will never eliminate death and taxes, his job is to drive down the number of customer complaints against his company as close to zero as possible.

1.0 Customer Complaints

1.1 Complaints come in many varieties: the costly, the inexpensive, the most frequent, the occasional, the major, the minor, and the inconvenient. All of them costly in terms of reduced profits and lost customers. Some complaints may not be viewed as complaints because they are handled on the phone when the customer calls. Others may be swept under the rug or not communicated to management (a big, big mistake. If the owner or manager isn't aware of the problem, trust me when I say it will not be resolved). In any respect, there will always be complaints. The measure of the trade contractor is how well he resolves them.

1.2 The typical trade contractor has a policy to resolve all complaints as cheaply as possible. That's understood; it's the nature of business. The owner or salesperson (often the same person) has the discretion to resolve those complaints. And it's often done informally, through the owner instructing his employees of corrective or preventive actions. But without a formal system to record and analyze complaints, management may not be aware of the extent of actual complaints, *and therefore not in a position to realize that customers may very well go shopping somewhere else for trade contactor services.* Nor can the owner take action to correct the root causes of complaints if he is unaware of them.

1.3 As with most companies, complaints that come to the attention of management are dealt with on a timely basis, but there may not be actions to assure that the root causes are determined, the problems resolved, and preventive action taken to prevent recurrences.

1.4 Unfortunately when a complaint comes to the attention of management, the response is often that somebody in the company gets an ass chewing. This does not work! When there is an ass chewing, the recipient closes his mind and hears little of what his supervisor says. He knows that he is in trouble, and the typical reaction is "I'm not to blame; it was . . ."

1.5 The process should focus on determining the root cause of the problem that caused the complaint and developing a plan to take corrective action and assess the results of the corrective action.

1.6 It is well-known that 80-85 percent of all quality problems are management correctable. They are caused by management's faulty control of the product, process, program, or employees' training and coaching. Instead, here are the type of questions that management should ask:

❖ Product or service. Is there a problem with the product or service?

❖ Process. Is there a problem with the process the company uses to deliver the service?

❖ Program. How is the service initiated? How does the company market its services? Does it make promises it cannot keep?

❖ Field site and equipment. Is there a problem with the facilities and the type of equipment needed to service customers?

❖ Employees. Is there a problem with the caliber of employees or their training?

Employee error accounts for the other ten to fifteen percent of quality problems. Frequently what is termed employee error is incomplete training of the employee or poor maintenance of equipment. These are not employee errors. They are training or maintenance problems, both of which are management responsibilities.

Corrective action planning is a tool for continuous improvement. The objective of a corrective action plan is to define the corrective action, assign responsibility for implementation, and provide for follow-up.

2.0 Corrective Action Plan (See example at the end of this section)

Use a corrective action plan to eliminate an unfavorable quality variance or to sustain a favorable quality variance. It has several parts. Each part must be included if the plan is to be effective. The parts are:

❖ Statement of the problem. Describe the problem in as much detail as possible.

❖ Root cause. Identify the root cause of the variance. Several common and easy-to-use techniques exist to identify root causes of problems . They are extensive, easy to use, but unfortunately beyond the purview of this book.

❖ Plan of action. This is the plan developed by the owner, manager, and employees to eliminate the variance.

❖ Responsible party. The employees(s) responsible for the implementation of the fixes.
❖ Suspense date. The date the action plan is scheduled for completion.
❖ Follow Up. Assigned to the employee responsible for following up to assure that the fix is implemented and working, with progress checked frequently by the company owner or his assigned representative.
❖ Form. The plan does not need to elaborate. A form like the one attached to this procedure is effective (Corrective Action Plan).

3.0 Summary

Corrective action planning is a tool for improvement. It provides a method to assure that the right corrective action is taken and at the right time. Corrective action planning is only as good as the follow-up.

4.0 Six Steps to Customer Enthusiasm

1. *Listen* to your customers. Don't assume; ask. Seek to understand their specific need, desires, and expectations.

2. Create an environment of *mutual trust*. Be caring and responsive to customer requests. Be honest and timely, and do not build false expectations.

3. Think in terms of *exceeding customer expectations*. Do what is right for the customer. Stand behind your products and services. Strive to go the extra step that transforms customer satisfaction into *customer enthusiasm*.

4. *Make it happen. Speed* is essential. Create a *win-win* culture and environment for the customer and the trade contractor both.

5. *Follow-up* with the customer to assure that the customer's expectations are met or exceeded.

6. Seek to *continually improve* the quality of your products and services in the eyes of your customers.

CORRECTIVE ACTION PLAN

PREPARED BY: _____ DATE: _____

STATEMENT OF PROBLEM:
_____

ROOT CAUSE:
_____

CORRECTIVE ACTION:
_____

ASSIGNED TO:
_____

SUSPENSE DATE: _____

FOLLOW UP BY_____

RESULTS:
_____

PURCHASING

Buying (purchasing) is not the act of picking up the phone and placing an order, nor is it giving the salesperson an order when he or she comes in to give you a pitch. Buying is both an art and a science, and it must be studied and learned if you want to buy the highest quality goods and services at the lowest possible cost.

1.0 You're Up Against Slick Willie

Salespeople have a bag of tricks they can and will use to get you to pay the highest possible price for their companies' goods and services. All with a smile and a slap on the back. Don't ever think salespeople don't have the skills to get their own sweet way. Most are consummate persuaders who are adept at overcoming the resistance of all but the most highly skilled buyers.

Fortunately, there is also a set of rules that the skilled buyer can use to neutralize the moves of even the slickest salespeople. Here they are, listed below.

2.0 Always Shop and Negotiate . . .Always

2.1. The successful sales person *always* shoots for a close at every available opportunity. Don't take the hook until you've shopped for the best deal possible, taking into account:

❖ Price, quantity, price break, quantity discounts, and freight rates.
❖ Service.
❖ Quality (make high quality non-negotiable).
❖ Benefits to your company.
❖ Discount policy and terms.

2.2 Negotiate with your suppliers.

2.3 Don't be an easy mark.

2.4 Don't allow yourself to be sold until you've checked and you are sure that you've obtained the lowest price possible for the highest quality goods and services available.

3.0 Buy Benefits, Service, Guarantees, and Quality

3.1 Competitively priced products and services may cost less *but* they may also offer less. Look beyond the salesperson's sales patter.

3.2 Purchase only from the company that will back up what it sells.

3.3 Negotiate the delivery service you require.

3.4 Don't be hooked by a nationally advertised name. An unknown supplier may offer better benefits, unless, in buying for resale, you absolutely *must* have that national brand.

3.5 Buy quality goods and services only. Never compromise on quality. Bad quality is expensive (scrap, rework, customer dissatisfaction). It drives away new buyers. Don't be caught being the last buyer to get stung before the word gets out to the grapevine.

3.6 A skilled salesperson will often sell the sizzle....not the steak. If you're buying steak, make sure that you're getting filet mignon, not hamburger helper.

4.0 Be Persistent

4.1 The successful salesperson is persistent, and will hang in until the sale is closed.

4.2 Make him come back to you . . . and check elsewhere before he gets back. You never know when a better deal will come your way. Do your homework.

5.0 Know Your Product and Service

5.1 Learn as much as you can about the products and services you purchase.

5.2 Learn the applications of the products and services.

5.3 Where there are specifications, learn the different specifications called for by   various companies and agencies and try, wherever possible, to purchase items   which   meet   the   most   stringent   of   those specifications.

5.4 Ask for samples and study them.

6.0 Know Thy Sales Representative

6.1 Understand that it is difficult to negotiate with complete strangers.

6.2 Learn the likes and dislikes of sales representatives. Know what makes them tick. They play the same game with you.

6.3 The successful salesperson will try to find the *button* that makes the buyer go. The successful buyer will attempt to find the sales representative's *button*, and push his first.

6.4 Set up a file on 3X5 index cards (or on your computer). For each salesperson collect this information:

> ❖ His name, company, products, likes and dislikes, hobbies, sports, and other interests. The object is to know whom you are dealing with.

❖ Note what subjects you discussed about the last time you talked.

❖ Briefly review the card before you talk to him again.

The sales representative will have the feeling that he is talking to a friend who remembers and cares about him as an important individual. As a result, the salesperson will be more likely to work to help you, the buyer.

6.5 It's not a bad idea to set up a similar file by company listing the customer service representatives. This group, as a whole, is normally treated as non-entities. When they are treated as if they matter, they will really bend over backwards for you.

7.0 Qualify the Sales Representative

7.1 When you negotiate, *don't* waste time by negotiating with the wrong person.

7.2 Make sure that the person with whom you negotiate *has the power* to negotiate.

7.3 If that person does *not* have the power, find out who does, and either talk to that person or send the representative back with your offer.

8.0 Know the Vendors

8.1 Know all of the potential suppliers for each of the products and services which your company requires.

8.2 Know which one you *can* use for your sources of supply, and know the ones which you *can't or don't want to*.

8.3 Know the competitors for each of your vendors.

8.4 Check the prices and deals with those competitors. Check often. In fact, check every time you need to buy goods or services.

8.5 You never know for sure unless you check which company may have changed its marketing strategies or may be attempting to cut back on inventories. You may be able to cut a beautiful deal.

8.6 *Don't* keep information in your head. Instead, keep a file on 3X5 cards (or on your computer) for vendors and products.

9.0 Conclusion

Buy quality, negotiate, and be persistent. Remember, buying is both a skill and an art, and over time you will become a quite capable buyer if you aren't already.

LOSS CONTROL

First, let's define loss control. It's what a company does to reduce its exposure to losses resulting from pilferage, fire, scrap, and anything else that produces an unnecessary financial loss. It also includes the specific methods applied by the company to reduce those risks. The purpose of the following operating procedure is to recommend implementation of a loss control and prevention program for the trade contractor's company that focuses on inventory shrinkage, the most prevalent loss normally encountered in the trade contractor's day-to-day business. The more job sites the company has the more its vulnerability to shrinkage.

1.0 Inventory Loss (shrinkage)
1.1 There are two basic sources of inventory loss we will address here. Shrinkage from:

- ❖ Vendors.
- ❖ Employees.

2.0 Shrinkage from Vendors
2.1 While the majority of a trade contractor's purchased parts and materials come from a few select vendors (not always the case but it's normal for a contractor to prefer certain vendors because of price, quality, or proximity), it is never too late to implement loss control measures. Successful vendors understand the need for controls.

- ❖ **Entrance to your building or job site**. Vendor shipments should be permitted to deliver through the *one* door or *one* spot at a job site only, and the truck driver should count each package or truckload of parts and materials in front of the assigned loss control employee (a trusted person working for the trade contactor).
- ❖ **Count**. When the parts and materials are counted, it is not uncommon for drivers to be very quick and run the count much faster than the loss control employee. The loss control employee should make sure he truly has counted the same number as the vendor, and not succumbed to pressure for a fast (and often inaccurate) count.
- ❖ **Packaging.** Items which come in boxes should have each box individually inspected as to contents. This should not upset the driver. If it does, request another driver from the

supplier. When counting products, be assured the cases are full. When receiving loose goods from a vendor, advise of discrepancies as soon as possible after delivery.

❖ **Lot codes.** When appropriate, expiration dates should be checked by the loss control employee regularly and set aside expired products for return to the vendor. For example, chemicals a window washing business uses that lose their potency after expiration dates. Do not rely on every vendor to rotate the stock without your loss control employee observing the process.

3.0 Shrinkage from Employees

❖ **Cash controls.** Basic fundamentals should be adhered to when allowing an employee to handle cash. Most of these controls center on the petty cash box, which depending on the size of the contractor's operations, could range up to several thousands of dollars over the course of a year.

    o The employee in charge of petty cash must be responsible for the beginning bank, all pay-outs from his drawer, and all receipts he has handled in his shift. In most trade contracting businesses, this will be the company's administrative employee.

    o Management should regularly spot check the employee in charge of petty cash. If this is done in an unscheduled fashion, the employee responsible for petty cash will never know if he is going to be audited and will be less prone to cheat. This raises the issue of trust. There's an old Italian proverb that's appropriate here. To trust is good; not to trust is better.

    o Employees other than the employee responsible for petty cash who steals from the petty cash drawer will generally do it if the patty cash box is unlocked and accessible. Locking the petty cash box and keeping it out of bounds for all but the employee assigned to handle petty cash will prevent this. Conducting spot check audits will keep this practice to a minimum.

    o Video cameras are very helpful in tracking employees' actions and duties. They are cheap and easy to install.

❖ **Purchases.** Any employee purchasing spare parts or materials from the company (for example, at a scrap sale), must keep the receipt attached to the package or bag at all times until he leaves company property. Employees purchasing parts and materials to take home, must purchase after their shift and directly before they leave. All merchandise must be purchased from management.

4.0   Vendor purchases

❖   Management must have in place a system of checks and balances to assure that those employees responsible for buying goods and services are not in bed with vendors. For example, buying goods and services from vendors for inflated prices and receiving kickbacks in return. It is beyond the scope of this book to describe such a system, but the company's accountant can help set one up with the help of the local police department.

5.0   Trash disposal

❖   No parts or materials are to be taken out to the trash without permission of management and the appropriate paperwork to indicate a scrapped item.

❖   All trash should be collected in clear bags, which will allow the contents to be viewed easily.

❖   If the rear door or rear gate of the contractor's business is used to take out trash, employees should not be allowed to park their cars in the rear of the property.

❖   Trash should not be allowed to be removed during the night shift. Bags must be left inside for disposal during the day.

❖   Field managers should occasionally inspect the dumpster to assure that employees are not dumping acceptable quality parts and materials. If the manager finds good parts and materials in the dumpster it could mean one of two things: Either employees do not understand the difference between acceptable and defective parts and materials (in which case they need to be re-educated) or that good parts and materials are being dumped during the day, and employees are returning at night to steal them and sell them elsewhere. In which case a strategically mounted video camera will record who they are and subject them to dismissal and possible arrest.

PART FIVE

METHODS FOR IMPROVING EMPLOYEE PERFORMANCE

Imagine the following scenario. You are a trade contractor who has struggled to remain profitable and stay in business. Finally, now that your business is starting to grow you feel you can take a week off to go to Hawaii; the first vacation you have taken in four years.

You return from a relaxing vacation and immediately call together your team to review the current project: building seventeen ranch homes in a new retirement community for seniors that will eventually have over three-hundred homes. A lot is riding on the success of this project. If you complete the project within the time schedule you will receive a contract to build even more homes.

Here is what you uncover at the meeting:

(1) Late lumber delivery. Enough to throw you off schedule and play overtime catch-up for the next two weeks. This failure was a result of your parts and materials supervisor not checking the posted receiving schedule.

(2) One of your workers fell off a scaffold and broke his leg. The work site supervisor was rushing him.

(3) The master builder is complaining about broken promises. Your manager doesn't know *what* promises.

(4) Your workers are grumbling about lax overtime pay and are threatening a walk-out.

Does any of this ring a bell? If you are the owner of a trade contracting business, you know exactly what I mean. Simply put, your employees are not living up to expectations. More often than not, their inadequacies are the result of insufficient direction on your part as well as the failure *on your part* to install employee systems that will identify the right people for the jobs and keep your employees functioning at high levels. The purpose of this section is to identify such systems. It covers these subjects:

Hiring and selection process

Employee compensation program

Progressive discipline

Performance evaluations

HIRING AND SELECTION PROCESS

A trade contractor can't find hard-working, capable employees without a hiring process that separates the loafers and incompetents from smart, hard workers. The following procedure will provide you with a way to screen out the worst and hire the best.

1.0 Hiring the Best Possible Job Candidates
1.1 This procedure is a general guideline for finding the best qualified employees.

2.0 Position Approval and Posting
2.1 The request for hiring new employees can originate from any of the company's managerial or supervisory employees.
2.2 A new job title requires a job description and the setting of a wage or salary range. The direct supervisor will prepare the job description for approval by the owner and may suggest a salary range for a new title.
2.3 Post approved job openings on the firm's bulletin board for one week before advertising jobs to the public. This gives current employees a first chance to seek advancement in the firm. Providing employees first crack at any new job opening helps build morale.
2.4 Advertise open positions outside the firm if no internal candidates are chosen in the first week. Use online job boards, employee referrals, professional industry contacts, employment agencies, or government job placement agencies to find potential candidates.

3.0 Selecting Job Candidates to Interview
3.1 Qualifications for the job determine how much experience a job candidate will need. *List those qualifications on a sheet of paper so you are always aware of what qualifications the job requires, and refer to it when interviewing job candidates.* Look for candidates that have the best qualifications you want and arrange to interview them.
3.2 There are several methods of screening multiple candidates who apply for jobs. It's not unusual in a depressed job economy to find literally hundreds of job applicants after a single advertised position, most of them out of work.

❖ In the ad you run in the newspaper or online job board, listing a telephone number instead of an address permits you to screen all candidates initially by telephone, if you only have time for a few onsite, personal interviews. Screen the calls by asking for major skills and experience to screen out the unqualified and bring in the few top candidates.

❖ To select from a pool of similar applicants, you might call them all in at once and explain the job to the entire group, then Interview them each separately. This is the fastest way to do it, but it requires all of the candidates to be physically present.

3.2   When candidates arrive for an interview, have them complete an application form *even when they provide resumes*. The application form provides several benefits:

❖ It collects the same information about every candidate in the same format. Some resumes omit information you need or desire.

❖ A well-designed application form provides space for the interviewer's comments.

❖ The application is the basis for employment and constitutes the job candidate's official and legal record. Should the applicant have lied or misled about previous jobs, he can be terminated, and the application used in any subsequent court battle.

4.0   Interviewing

4.1   The prepared interviewer will have with him:

❖ The job description, including a list of desired qualifications.

❖ A list of questions to ask and topics to cover. He should ask the same questions of each and every job candidate. He doesn't have to ask them in the same order, but he should cover the same ground to eliminate prejudicial thinking or bias.

❖ A score sheet listing what he is looking for in an outstanding candidate, which he will complete to compare the candidates by category.

4.2   You need to uncover this type of information when evaluating a candidate:

❖ Skills, education, and experience. The employment application should help you evaluate the candidate's measurable qualifications, and you should review those because his previous work experience case may differ, and it is important that you understand those differences. For example, a job candidate may have built commercial buildings at another trade contractor's company, but he may not be fully experienced in your requirements for constructing homes.

❖ Motivation and positive attitude. These are qualifications which are difficult to identify except through an examination of work examples from the applicant's pervious jobs, or from personal references. Look carefully for signs that the applicant may be a problem later on. You are not required to hire someone who won't meet your firm's standards for quality and teamwork . . . and you shouldn't. This is often the more difficult of the evaluation criteria, but the hardest to determine because, as we all know, job candidates *always* present a "pretty face."

❖ Is the candidate trainable, willing to follow directions, a hard worker? Ask for examples of what he learned and how he feels about learning new things. See if you can determine how he handled unexpected situations. For example, did he consult with his boss and fellow employees or did he try to solve problems unassisted? What you're trying to uncover here is the lone wolf. Lone wolves don't work well in the pack, and the worst thing is to hire an employee who won't work as a team member.

❖ If specific examples don't help you make your decision, you may find it useful to try direct questions such as: Why did you choose this line of work? What about it do you like now? Give five characteristics that describe you as a worker. Why do you want to leave your present job? What do you want in a job that you aren't getting now?

4.3 Be enthusiastic and positive during the interview. You represent the firm to this applicant, and you must project a good image. You don't want a candidate you've selected to turn you down!

4.4 Let the candidate ask questions. Decide what you want every candidate to know, and what you don't wish to discuss. He probably would like to know if the firm is growing, what the hours are, and other job-related questions.

4.5 If the applicant volunteers any personal facts not related to information discussed above, interrupt and remind him that the interview is confined to job-related information, and only that information will be used in the final hiring decision.

4.6 Clearly state the next steps in the selection process for the candidate. Close an interview with a handshake, even if it didn't go very well.

4.7 Contact at least one reference for any candidate you are considering seriously to assure confirmation of his abilities and professionalism. Speak to a former supervisor, not a human resources representative (assuming the trade contractor is large enough to have such a position), whenever possible.

- ❖ Some employers will be reluctant to give candid opinions about a former employee, and will only confirm facts such as the dates of an employee's employment period. There is always the concern that the job candidate may sue his former employer if his failure to land the job was because of a poor reference.
- ❖ Even from such employers, if you read between the lines, your questions should turn up some information about the candidate's performance. *Do more listening than talking.*
- ❖ Questioning references should include the basics: Confirm the job title and employment period. Ask about attendance, initiative, and overall performance. Ask if the former employer would rehire the job candidate. Listen carefully. This can be a very revealing question.

4.8 Rate each candidate on how well you believe he would perform the primary duties of the job based on his qualifications and trainability. Select the person whom you believe will exceed the performance requirements of the job. Hire the best!

4.9 Determine when the candidate can start work, and prepare an orientation for his first few days of work.

4.10 Legal constraints

- ❖ Federal law regulates the types of questions you can ask during an interview. For example, Title VII of the 1964 Civil Rights Act prohibits discrimination based on race, sex, color, national origin, and religion. The Age Discrimination in Employment Act prohibits questions about a person's age. The Americans with Disabilities Act of 1990, among other things, protects qualified individuals with disabilities from discrimination in employment.

❖ Avoid questions relating either directly or indirectly to age, sex, race, color, national origin, religion, or disabilities.

❖ If information you need about an applicant potentially infringes on any of the above categories, be sure the question relates to an occupational qualification or is required by law to be asked. *Check first with the company's lawyer.*

❖ The company owner and other members of management should be aware of some of the specific prohibitions imposed by the enactment of the Americans with disabilities Act. For example:

   o Employers may NOT inquire about an applicant's workers compensation history during the pre-offer stage.

   o Employers may NOT ask if an applicant has a disability.

   o Employers MAY ask if there is anything that precludes the applicant from performing the essential functions of the position for which he is applying.

   o The interviewer should go over the essential functions of the position with the applicant so he has the information needed to make that determination. Use the job description as a crutch.

❖ All members of management who conduct interviews should be well-versed in federal and state laws that regulate the types of questions that may be raised in an employment interview.

❖ Whenever an employee of the Company is not sure if a question violates federal or state legislation, he is better off not asking the question and checking with the company owner who can then ask his legal counsel.

5.0 Interviewing Summary

5.1 You're looking for potential employees who are flexible and willing to make things happen as supportive, team players.

5.2 In advertising, interviewing, and conducting performance reviews, always adhere to objective, job-related issues.

6.0 Timeline

6.1 The following timeline may help you organize your hiring process. Although this procedure was drafted for a larger trade contractor's company, the concept still applies to smaller operations (albeit on a shrunken time period). The essential task is to follow the steps, even when you compress the time period.

	Target Date	Duration	Task
1	_____	0 days	Identify hiring need.
2	_____	0-2 days	Prepare position guide for new position.
3	_____	2-5 days	Evaluate job, salary range, budget.
4	_____	1 day	Owner approves job request.
5	_____	7 days	Post position internally one week.
6	_____	2 days	Prepare ad or online notice.
7	_____	2 days	Arrange for publicity; place ad.
8	_____	2 days	Prepare interview questions.
9	_____	3 - 7 days	Review responses, select candidates for interviews.
10	_____	1 - 2 days	Call candidates and arrange appointments.
11	_____	1-14 days	Conduct interviews, rank candidates.
12	_____	1-2 days	Check references of top choice.
13	_____	1 day	Select candidate.
14	_____	1-14 days	Candidate starts work.

Total time elapsed before starting work: 18 - 20 days. Smaller trade contractor companies may very well compress this cycle. The important point is to follow the steps.

7.0 Candidate Evaluation Checklist

7.1 When conducting the interview use the candidate evaluation checklist shown on the following page:

CANDIDATE EVALUATION CHECKLIST

Which candidate will be able to do an outstanding performance in this job? (Rate from 1-4 with 4 being the highest or most desirable, 1 the least desirable.

Candidate				
Date Interviewed				
Notes				
Skills/Experience . List below:				
1.				
2.				
3.				
4.				
5.				
6. Education				
7. Team Player				
8. Commitment to Quality				
9. (Write in)				
Totals Points				
Other Notes				
When Available				
Salary Desired				

Evaluator: _____
Choice: _____
Comments: _____

EMPLOYEE COMPENSATION PROGRAM

When it comes to trade contractors motivating their employees, nothing is as important as the employee compensation plan. Sure, employees expect to be treated fairly and equitably, but first they have to bring home the bacon to mama and the kids. That's basic, and unfortunately too many trade contractors, involved with the technical side of their businesses, fail to consider their employee's basic needs. The result is high turnover, and high turnover is expensive. Allow me to suggest a compensation program that will help your business succeed.

1.0 An Employee Compensation Program That Works

1.1 This standard procedure outlines employee compensation policies for trade contractors.

1.2 Fair and equitable pay for prompt, timely, and accurate performance of assigned tasks and responsibilities is a major premise of the employee/employer relationship. Each employee contributes to the success of the business.

1.3 The company owner or his representative is responsible for the establishment and administration of wages, salaries, commissions, and bonuses.

2.0 Concept of the Program

2.1 Control of payroll costs is the responsibility of management. The owner or his representative is responsible for administering the wage, salary, and bonus program.

2.2 Positions in the organization are developed to fulfill a function for the business. All employee functions have an economic value.

2.3 The company's organization chart is used to help determine each employee's economic value. There may be special circumstances relating to a position and its economic value that fall outside this guideline, but if so it's an exception to the rule.

2.4 *Any position on the organization chart is only worth so much money to the company.* It makes no difference who fills the position or for how long. For example, it doesn't make economic sense to pay laborers the same money made by the company's managers. But it may make sense to pay a highly skilled specialist more than a manager, especially if that specialist's skills are essential to the company's success and in high demand in the marketplace

2.5   Base pay is the floor amount that the job is worth to the company. In the case of workers, the job's worth is normally quoted in dollars per hour. For managerial and technical employees their jobs may sometimes be expressed in dollars per week or per month.

2.6   Special cases may be found in the organization but all pay is still based on performance of some kind. If there are too many such special cases, then something is wrong with the company's compensation plan and needs to be corrected. Nothing is so demoralizing to employees as unequal pay for the same job.

2.7   The board of directors determines management salaries, pre-planned profits, and the percent of profits to be distributed through the bonus or incentive plan.

2.8   Pay schedules are reviewed annually and updated by management. In the case of a management-union contract, pay rates for union workers are dictated by negotiations.

❖ All non-union employee pay rates are reviewed annually, as a minimum, on the anniversary or hire date, and in conjunction with the annual survey of wages for range and upon the merit value of duties and responsibilities assumed. All changes in pay rate are reflected in the annual budget and all pay discussions or changes are logged in the employee's personnel folder.

3.0   Compensation Procedure

3.1   The company owner or his representative will develop the base rate schedule for each position, taking the following steps:

❖ Identify each employee position within the company.
❖ Call the following organizations and companies for current pay information:
   o Local job service center.
   o Local chamber of commerce.
   o Local competitors.
   o Local college placement office.
   o Local associations.
   o National associations of trade contractors.
   o State reference sources.
❖ Obtain the following: high, low, and average pay rate for the comparable company position, while providing the source of the information. (See *Wage and Salary Survey* at the end of this section.)
❖ Average the above wage and salary information to create your anticipated wage and salary ranges for each position.

❖ Update wage and salary information gathered at appropriate times, such as an annual review or whenever someone calls for salary information, someone quits for a better paying job.

3.2 Hire new employees at the bottom of the wage or salary range. The company owner may hire exceptional candidates at a higher rate at his discretion, such as for a worker with hard-to-find skills, although this practice, if used extensively, can cause dissension among employees.

3.3 Based on an employee evaluation, the wage or salary may be increased within the year. The new rate will not exceed the top of the range.

3.4 Each year the company owner will, through personal observations and discussions with the management team, rank all employees and compare their positions against a wage or salary range scale. The information provided will form the basis for wage adjustment from other than promotion or increased responsibilities.

3.5 Based on continued acceptable evaluations, an employee's wages may be increased after each one year of employment, but not to exceed the maximum for the position.

3.6. The wages and salaries of the trade contractor's company must not exceed the maximum for the position in any event. Once an employee reaches the top value in the wage range, no salary increases are possible unless the wage and salary schedule changes. Any additional earnings realized by the employee must be the result of the employee accepting more responsibilities and is the equivalent of a promotion to a new job title and wage range.

3.7 When the economy tanks, the company may need to reduce the schedule. This is accomplished by not hiring employees for the same functional position at the previous wage scale.

4.0 Employee Wages

4.1 The employee's wage structure will be determined annually by the company owner or his representative subsequent to an in-depth wage survey.

4.2 The owner and managers will be responsible for the review and recommendation of the wage rate for all employees. The standing rates for new employees will depend on their levels of experience, education, and ability.

4.3 Wages will be paid weekly based on the satisfactory completion of assigned tasks and responsibilities.

5.0   Summary

5.1   Asking other sources for information about their current wage and salary carries the responsibility to share your wage and salary information with those same organizations.

5.2   All of the trade contractor's wage and salary ranges should be reviewed and updated where required annually, as a minimum, prior to the start of the new fiscal year.

5.3   All non-union employees' pay should be reviewed annually, at a minimum, with the employee at the time of budget development.

5.4   Wages may go down as well as up. That depends on the local economy and union contract. By keeping the wage and salary rates current and the employees informed, there will be no surprises.

WAGE AND SALARY SURVEY

Position: Framing Supervisor   Date of Survey: _____
(Complete one survey for each different category)
ABC, Incorporated Current Wage Range: _____
Number of Employees in this category: _____

SURVEY RESULTS

List Company names or source of data	No. of Employees	Average Pay	Top Pay	Minimum Pay

PROGRESSIVE DISCIPLINE

One of the most unpleasant tasks a manager faces is disciplining employees. Yet, without discipline (See below *2.0 Defining a System* for a definition of discipline) in the ranks of the trade contractor's company, the performance of employees inevitably slips and with it company profits. As the old saying goes, "A few bad apples spoil the barrel." Allow one or more employees to ignore company rules and before you know it, that bad attitude spills over to other normally good employees. If nothing else, good employees lose faith in company managers and morale drops.

The inevitable conclusion is that discipline is required. How it's conducted is another issue that is addressed in the following procedure.

1.0 Discipline Matters

1.1 The purpose of this standard procedure is to establish and define a system of disciplinary policies and procedures, for this organization, that will govern the actions of all employees.

1.2 All employment and compensation is "at will." "At will" means that employment can be terminated with or without cause, and with or without notice, at any time, at the option of the company owner or his managers, except as otherwise provided by law. Nothing in this procedure is intended to change employment-at-will.

2.0   Defining a System

2.1   In any organization, discipline must be maintained at all times. Discipline should not, however, be considered a tool with which to punish employees. Instead, discipline should be viewed as a positive, reinforcing, corrective process that when used properly can correct an employee's wrongful behavior.

2.2   In order to assure that correction, rather than punishment, is the guidepost to an organization's disciplinary policy, the disciplinary system should be influenced by the following principles:

❖ There must be made available to all employees, clear, articulated work rules, policies, and procedures that are to be followed without exception (unless otherwise determined by company management).

❖ A system of oral and written warnings must be devised and implemented that will provide employees with a clear and unmistakable notice that further misbehavior can result in more extreme discipline and ultimately termination.

❖ A disciplined employee must be involved fully in the disciplinary process. This includes both a thorough hearing of the employee's side of the story, and a declaration in writing from the employee stating methods he will use to correct the unacceptable behavior.

❖ Thorough and complete documentation throughout every step of the disciplinary process is absolutely necessary to provide both a record of the disciplinary steps that are taken and to inform the employee with a clear, written notice of the problem that must be corrected.

2.3   It goes without saying, that when corrective action fails, discharge of the errant employee is warranted and required. *Not to do so sends an unmistakable message to other employees that bad behavior is acceptable.*

3.0   Establishing Company Work Rules

3.1   While contractual language is important, it is an organization's written work rules that govern day-to-day life in the workplace. It is usually a violation of one or more of these rules or regulations that results in a disciplinary action or discharge being brought against an employee. Therefore, particular care must be given to the development, implementation, and maintenance of a proper, efficient, and well-written set of work rules, regulations, policies, and procedures.

3.2   A proper and efficient disciplinary system is built on the principle of *employee awareness*. Communication regarding work rules is very important. Therefore, all employees must be given a copy of the published work rules. In addition, each employee must sign a form acknowledging they have received the work rules and have read them. In addition, an employer must have a process established and functioning that efficiently notifies employees of any changes in the established rules or regulations in a timely manner. This can be accomplished, for example, through the use of paycheck flyers, at employee meetings, or with a central communications system, such as a bulletin board or similar device. In this regard, notices enclosed with an employee's paycheck act much like a "signed receipt" for changes in work rules.

3.3   Management must also build a degree of flexibility into the work rules, such as allowing cross reinforcement of established work rules. For example, if an employee is at the written warning level for three or four different types of misconduct, there should be latitude given to use separate, specific types of wrongful conduct in tandem, to suspend, or even discharge, the errant employee.

4.0   Imposing Discipline

4.1   To properly correct employee behavior and to enforce reasonable work rules and regulations, management must have a written, positive, or progressive disciplinary system in effect. In addition, management must make sure that the system is applied evenly throughout the entire organization. It may be pointed out that the physical act of instituting a disciplinary system is most important to the efficient operation of the organization as a whole. Equally important, is the methodology involved in the operation of the system once it's installed. The following is a step-by-step review of an accepted and efficient disciplinary system that can serve as a guide to establishing your own progressive disciplinary system.

4.2   The verbal warning

❖   A verbal warning is generally given when an employee *first* violates a particular rule, regulation, policy, or procedure. The matter is usually addressed between the immediate supervisor and the employee. The supervisor informs the employee that he has violated company rules and that a written notice is being placed in his personal file.

❖   Even at the verbal warning stage the employee must always be given the opportunity to tell his side of the story. In addition, any disciplinary action or warning form that is used must contain a space for the employee to respond, in writing, to any charges made against him. The employee does not admit guilt or innocence when adding comments or by simply signing a disciplinary action form. By signing the disciplinary action form, an employee is only acknowledging the fact that he is has been counseled to help improve his behavior.

❖   Equally useful, will be a space provided on the disciplinary action form where the employee is provided an opportunity to indicate how he is to correct the improper behavior that has been documented. This process involves more that the employee simply promising to try to improve, or giving lip service to a plan for improvement. To be totally effective, the employee must provide a written outline of the specific steps that he will undertake to correct his errant behavior. Further, the supervisor must follow-up closely on the intentions and actions of the employee and must document, in writing, any progress (or lack of progress) that the employee is making, or has made, toward actually correcting his behavior. All of this writing has two main purposes: to show the employee that the company means business, and to serve as a record in the event of further disciplinary action.

❖ Positive feedback, or the type described above, has several purposes.

- o Should the disciplined employee disagree with the action taken against him, management will learn of the reasons for the employee's disagreement immediately.

- o The disciplined employee is compelled to state his position early on in the disciplinary process. By doing so, the employee may then be unable to change his story later on.

- o Involving the employee in the entire disciplinary process allows him a real opportunity to be involved in correcting his behavior.

- o If the disciplined employee is ultimately discharged, it provides a solid foundation for management to defend its position. This is especially true, in a case where the employee agreed with management's earlier actions but failed to take the corrective action steps that were agreed to in order to correct his behavior.

- o The disciplined employee is given a chance to vent any ill feelings that may have arisen regarding the disciplinary action that was taken against him at an earlier stage. This action alone could very well head off any further action on the employee's part, including the filing of a grievance.

4.3   The written warning

❖ A written warning is simply a more formalized version of the verbal warning discussed above. A written warning makes it much clearer that the employee has violated a company rule, regulation, policy, or procedure, and that discipline will either be imposed immediately, or, if further misconduct occurs, will most certainly be imposed with harsher consequences at some later date.

❖ The supervisor, at this stage of the disciplinary process, should review the warning with the owner or next senior level manager in the company, prior to meeting with the employee to review the matter at hand. Again, give a copy of the warning to the employee at the conclusion of the meeting. The signed original form is to be placed in the employee's permanent personal file under lock and key for safekeeping.

❖ As with the verbal warning, give the disciplined employee the opportunity to state, in writing, his agreement or disagreement with the disciplinary action that has been imposed on him, and to state, in writing also, the specific actions that the employee will take to correct the behavior that has been identified.

4.4   Suspension or decision making leave

❖ Suspension, or decision-making leave, is not to be taken lightly by an employee who is being disciplined. Higher echelon management must be involved at his stage of the disciplinary process.

❖ Of key concern is whether the disciplinary leave will be paid or unpaid. Unpaid leave, obviously, acts as a punishment. Paid leave, on the other hand, is becoming an increasingly acceptable alternative, particularly as it relates to decision-making leave.

    o   Paid leave serves the purpose of leaving it up to the employee as to whether he actually wants to improve his behavior and return to work. The disciplined employee can decide to work within the system *or leave the company.*

    o   Before returning to work, the employee must again complete the company's disciplinary forms and indicate, in writing, his agreement with the disciplinary actions that have been taken by the company on his behalf.

4.5   Discharge

❖ If all else fails, the final step under any positive or progressive disciplinary system is discharge. However, before taking this final step, management must undertake a thorough investigation of the incident leading to discharge. The investigation must include the measures described below.

    o   There must be proper documentation. It cannot be stressed enough that every step of the disciplinary process must be reduced to some type of written document. In addition, the disciplined employee's signature should appear on each document.

    o   Management should obtain written statements or affidavits from any witnesses to the disciplined employee's misconduct.

    o   Outside legal counsel should review the basis for a discharge prior to taking final action. Often, it has been found that management officials do not conduct a sufficiently thorough investigation of the facts surrounding a discharge incident, and simply rely on the immediate supervisor's version of events leading to the discharge. *In all cases involving a discharge, a thorough, objective, efficient, and timely investigation of the discharge incident is a mandatory act that is to be conducted by the owner or qualified managers.*

    o   After conducting a thorough investigation of a pending discharge, and after the discharge has been executed, conduct an exit interview with the discharged person, if at all possible. During this exit interview, give the discharged person an opportunity to make any final comments regarding the discharge and to have the discharge fully explained to him. Again, comments and instructions must be placed in writing, a copy given to the discharged person and the originals placed in the discharged person's personal file, where it will be saved for as long as required.

4.6   Important points

❖ Two final points that must be kept in mind concerning disciplinary procedures and discharges are as follows:

     o Management must have the ability, under its disciplinary system, to bypass certain disciplinary steps. Flexibility should exist to match the seriousness of the offense with the proper disciplinary response.

     o Management must take time to thoroughly inform and assure the full understanding of all employees concerning the workings of the disciplinary system they put into place.

5.0   Establishing a Grievance Procedure

5.1   Contracts, or other types of written agreements, that are drawn between the company and an employee (or the company and a labor union), and the written company human resources policies in general, must always contain strict time limits regarding the filing and processing of a worker's grievance. Moreover, the language of these documents should restrict the discretion of an arbitrator to forgive failure to follow specified contractual or normal time limits. Additionally, the grievant should be required to outline, in writing, and on an authorized form, valid reasons as to why the organization's disciplinary action is inappropriate.

5.2   The establishment and enforcement of the above stated grievance provisions would serve to accomplish the following objectives:

❖ Potential grievance issues will surface immediately.

❖ It is less likely that employees will be frustrated by management's actions if they have an opportunity to respond to the actions that have been taken, showing that the matters are not neglected.

5.3   When investigating a potential discharge, a critical element that must be present is the interview of the offending employee. Specifically, management must give an employee the opportunity for legal or professional representation at a disciplinary interview. This is only true, however, if the employee requests such representation and the interview is, in fact, one that could lead to discipline or discharge. Failure to follow these rules could result in an unfair labor practice suit being filed on behalf of the employee against the organization.

6.0   Equal Application of the Rules

6.1   A key element in the investigation of any discharge is determining how management has handled similar cases in the past. If management, for example, has not discharged an employee previously for engaging in the same misconduct, a later attempt to discharge an employee for that same misconduct may very well be challenged and disallowed by a judge or labor arbitrator.

6.2   Similarly, management must review whether the same employee engaged in misconduct previously. If any evidence of prior misconduct is found, what disciplinary action, if any, was taken the previous times? If an employee has not been disciplined previously, even though he has engaged in improper conduct, a sudden change in management's approach to discipline may very well be questioned if a judge or arbitrator reviews the incident.

6.3   There are several precautionary steps that management may take in order to limit the effects, or the impact, of any inconsistent disciplinary action. These steps are discussed as follows:

❖ As previously noted, the company must have written rules, regulations, policies, and procedures that provide for latitude in imposing discipline. If management has some discretion over the penalties it might impose, one could very well differentiate the present case from the former cases and not be locked into a precedent.

❖ Another option available is for management to obtain a waiver from the employee if it decides that a rule will not be strictly enforced and some relief is to be granted to the employee who violates such a rule. This can be accomplished through the use of a form that indicates that management's actions are not to be considered as precedent setting by any outside review or regulatory agency.

❖ Management has yet another option, which is to offer the offending employee a last chance letter prior to discharge. In this process, the employee simply agrees to go on probation for a specified period of time. In return, management will not discharge the employee for the particular offense under review. However, any further offenses on the part of the employee will result in immediate discharge without the right to arbitrate or to invoke any other recourse.

❖ It must be stated that even through the above tactics may be used effectively, management should rarely make exceptions to established disciplinary rules, regulations, policies, and procedures.

The more exceptions that are made, the more likely is the reality that a disciplinary action taken by management will be overturned if subjected to formal review, the entire system will be weakened, and eventually the system will be totally ineffective.

7.0   The Importance of Documentation

7.1   A common theme present throughout this procedure has been the importance of proper and complete documentation in every step of the disciplinary process. It has been proven in case after case, that the primary cause of an employee discharge being overturned is the lack of pertinent documentation.

7.2   Documentation, however, is not only vital from the standpoint of supporting management's disciplinary or discharge actions, it is also useful in letting employees know what it is they have done in error, and what can happen to them if their conduct is not corrected in a very short period of time. In other words, the employee is provided with a written explanation of his misconduct and in addition, is given clear instructions as to what must be done to correct misconduct and the consequence of any further misconduct.

7.3   Each step of the disciplinary process must be documented. A good rule to place into effect is that *all verbal warnings must be recorded in writing.* A verbal warning that is not written down could well result in a credibility conflict between the disciplined employee and the immediate front-line supervisor who is most likely administering the discipline.

7.4   The corrective nature of the system, along with flexibility, fairness, and documentation, are keys to an efficient and effective discharge when required. If management stresses corrective action with documentation throughout the entire disciplinary process, the company should be able to successfully defend a challenge by a regulatory agency or the union.

8.0   Conclusion

8.1   By closely following the guidelines described in this standard procedure, management will be more assured that its decision to discharge an employee will be upheld and not overturned if a formal review is held regarding the incident.

8.2   The company must select an efficient disciplinary form and put it into effect as soon as possible if such a form is not already in effect. In addition, the company must assure that all managers and supervisors are thoroughly indoctrinated in the correct use of the entire disciplinary system, including all required forms.

PERFORMANCE EVALUATIONS

The purpose of this standard procedure is to describe the rationale, benefits and procedures for employee evaluations at ABC Contracting. The evaluation forms included with this standard procedure are designed to provide a practical method of measuring the performance of employees, both in qualitative and quantitative terms.

1.0 Background to Employee Evaluations
1.0 Employee evaluations, when used constructively, are useful tools for:

- ❖ Recognizing satisfactory and excellent performance.
- ❖ Improving unsatisfactory performance and undesirable behavior.
- ❖ Providing a basis for meritorious pay increases and promotions.
- ❖ Evaluating the performance of recently hired employees.
- ❖ Determining the reaction of employees to recent position changes.
- ❖ Determining the potential of employees for reclassification or promotion.
- ❖ Determining which employees to layoff or furlough, when necessary.
- ❖ Developing or maintaining employee incentive and bonus programs.

2.0 Purpose and Concepts of an Evaluation Procedure
2.1 The Company should use a semi-annual evaluation system because, in the normal working day, discussions generally concern job-related problems. Usually an employee's personal qualities are only discussed when there is a problem, but not when performance is satisfactory. Using an evaluation program will force the company to objectively form judgments about employee performance, and thereby take the actions necessary to improve overall company performance.

2.2 Employee evaluations are a means for evaluating the performance of employees and noting areas for improvement or commendation. The purpose of the company evaluation system is also to provide the company with a practical quantitative and qualitative measure of the abilities of employees, and a practical measure of the progress of each individual.

2.3 Employee evaluations are a means for positive improvement. When done properly and thoroughly, the process becomes a powerful mechanism for the improvement of employees and their productivity.

2.4 The evaluation system should be viewed as a positive process. Both the employee and the supervisor performing the evaluation sometimes misunderstand this. The evaluation program is intended to be positive and constructive for employees, their supervisors and the company. While evaluation has a certain negative connotation, the intent is not to find fault, but to develop better employees and a better company.

2.5 Employee evaluations provide a vehicle for better communication. It is natural for a supervisor to form an opinion or judgment of each employee. In turn, the employee has formed an opinion of the quality of supervision and the quality of work that he performs. Very often these views are quite different. The review portion of the evaluation system helps to minimize the differences in these sincerely held opinions. Both the employee and the supervisor will then more clearly understand their working relationship as well as what is and what isn't acceptable performance.

2.6 The evaluation process should improve employee productivity. Most employees want to do a good job. The evaluation procedure is one way of discussing whether the employee can work more effectively and not necessarily harder.

3.0 Timing

3.1 As a general rule, conduct evaluations of new employees every thirty days for the first three months of their employment.

3.2 Conduct evaluations of full-time employees every six months based upon the date of their previous evaluation, although many companies frequently perform this evaluation once a year. It is up to the discretion of the company owner as to which he chooses. Trade contractors do both. The worst thing is to *not* have an evaluation system.

3.3 Evaluate employees promoted to new jobs every thirty days for the first three months of their promotion.

3.4 Evaluate employees receiving an evaluation score below average or standard every thirty days until their performance reaches a satisfactory or acceptable level.

3.5 Evaluate employees not promoted, but placed in other jobs as new employees, (every thirty days for the first three months).

4.0 Evaluation Considerations

4.1   Trade contracting management and employees must take evaluations seriously. Careless ratings will do permanent damage and are worse than no evaluation ratings at all.

4.2   Always base the evaluation on personal judgment, never on the comments of other people. Performance evaluations must be based on the supervisor's own observations and judgment.

4.3   Disregard any overall impressions and focus on one point at a time. *Supervisors should evaluate employees on each item or ability separately*, not on their overall impression of the individual.

4.4   Never base evaluations on one unusual event. Base evaluations on the typical day-to-day performance, not on extraordinary or extreme situations.

4.5   Always be sure to use maximum thought and care to assure fair and honest opinions.

4.6   Base pay increases on merit and performance as indicated by a review of recent evaluations. Merit and performance should be judged strictly on the basis of the regularly scheduled employee evaluations. Seniority and length of time on the job should have nothing to do with pay raises, unless otherwise specified in a management-union agreement.

4.7   Base promotions and terminations on merit, performance, and potential or the lack thereof. Review previous employee evaluations carefully before making decisions.

4.8   Discuss every evaluation with the employee preferably at the time the evaluation is conducted. Every employee must also have the opportunity to make his own comments about the evaluation, both verbally and in writing. This does not mean an evaluation will be changed. Formal written comments should be filed with the original copy of the evaluation.

4.9   Each employee must sign the evaluation and be given a copy during the evaluation interview.

4.10   To be effective in evaluating performance and correcting problems and to assure a constructive interview without the suggestion or appearance of personal bias, the reviewer must not be accusatory, prejudicial, vindictive, hostile, negative, or in any way emotional.

5.0 Discussion and Signing of Forms

5.1   Employees, especially key managers, may be requested to do a self-evaluation, in addition to the one done by their immediate supervisors. Always allow ample time to review the self-appraisals before scheduling the performance review. If an employee is too critical of his own performance (because of a short time in a new position, perhaps) you will want to praise the positive aspects that you have witnessed. Conversely, if an employee over-evaluates, this must be addressed with specific examples during the interview to make sure the employee or manager understands the seriousness of the evaluation process. Correct any perception the employee is better than his performance indicates.

    5.2   Show every employee evaluation to the employee and discuss it with him. The rational for this is:

- ❖ If the employee is not aware of the evaluation, the whole purpose of correcting and improving identified areas is defeated.
- ❖ Every employee must be provided the opportunity to make his own comments about the evaluation, both verbally and in writing. This does mean that an evaluation will be changed. Formal written comments by the manager and the evaluator are included with the appraisal and filed in the employee's personnel folder.
- ❖ Each employee must sign the evaluation following the interview and should be given a copy. Failure to sign (indicating that the evaluation form has been read and understood, even if not agreed to), may be considered insubordination and grounds for disciplinary action.

6.0 Performance Ratings

    Typical performance measurements for employees include productivity, quality, customer service, scrap and rework, absenteeism/tardiness, cost effectiveness, and a host of other criteria depending on the specific job. The point is that each company must devise its own employee evaluation system by defining the characteristics it wants measured, then evaluating each employee according to those measurements. For an idea of what an evaluation form would look like, see the candidate evaluation checklist in the section titled *Hiring and Selection Process*.

    The performance evaluation is based on 100 points for each characteristic measured. The employee's score is based on the total points arrived at by adding up all of the point values for the characteristics measured and dividing that number by the total number points possible. For example, a carpenter at a building site might be evaluated on these characteristics and have the following scores as determined by his supervisor (simplified and truncated for this example):

Measurement	Points	Top Points
Productivity	65	100
Quality of work	85	100
Customer service	80	100
Final rating 230/300(total possible points)= 77%	**230**	**300**

Interpret percentage scores as outlined below:

40 - 49 Employees scoring this low should be dismissed. Their performance is far too low and chances for improvement are marginal.

50 - 59 Employees scoring in this range are considered marginal. They should be informed that without improvement on their next evaluations, consideration will be given for dismissal. Re-evaluate this employee in 30 days.

60 - 69 This is the range of low to average performance. Many employees will score in this range. Improvement should be expected over the course of several evaluations. If this evaluation program is used in conjunction with an annual compensation program, this is the lowest scoring range for which pay increases may be justified, and then only if improvements in performance have taken place since past evaluations.

70 - 79 This is the range for average performance. Most employees will score in this range. Slow but steady improvement should be expected over several evaluations. The employees in this range should receive the average pay raise.

80 - 89 Evaluations in this range are very desirable. Employees scoring in this range demonstrate a high degree of involvement, performance, and drive. Above average pay increases at this level are advisable to encourage continued good performance and to recognize and reward past performance.

90 -100 This is the highest level of performance. Few employees will score consistently at this level, but it can be expected from the top performers. If this evaluation is used in conjunction with an annual compensation program, pay increases should be highest at this level. Employees scoring in this range should be groomed for advancement.

7.0 Summary

7.1   The employee evaluation system provides a fair and equitable means of measuring the performance of all employees. Each evaluation will contribute as a basis for rewarding deserving employees with more money or benefits. It will also assist in selecting employees for promotion.

7.2   If an employee has the skills necessary to satisfactorily perform the job but is not performing to expectations, the evaluation and interview will provide the means of salvaging the employee.

7.3   When you, the evaluator, have followed all the steps of an effective evaluation and coached and trained the employee to do his job, and provided ample time for improvement but there has been little or no measurable progress, then you must make a decision to:

❖   Reassign the employee to a job the employee can do, or

❖   Fully document the non-performance and terminate the employee.

PART SIX

MARKETING TRADE CONTRACTOR SERVICES

Let's talk about the intersection of trade contractors and social networking websites. Frankly, that intersection either doesn't exist for most trade contractors or they're aware of it but they haven't yet paid much attention to its marketing potential.

They should because they'll find discussion groups springing up all over the Internet that will help them learn new methods to improve their operations and find sales leads in their own backyards. They'll connect with trade contractors and subcontractors across the country and across the world. The beauty of it is if, for example, you're a paving company contractor operating your business in New Hampshire and you don't want to share trade secrets or customer leads with other pavers in your neighborhood, you won't mind doing so with pavers in California or Iowa. And you can learn a lot from other contractors who experience the same problems you have and know how to exploit the same opportunities.

As starters, you might consider joining *contractortalk.com* and asking other contractors how they get their new business leads or what kind of advertising works best for them or how they handle technical or business problems you've encountered. The possibilities are endless. Simply go to Google or Yahoo! and type in a phrase such as "sales leads for contractors" and you will be amazed at the staggering amount of information available . . . information to help your business succeed and flourish. Here are two others I selected at random: *http://bu-construction-industry.co.cc/* and *http://www.contractorpromarketing.com/*, or if you're in the roofing business as an example, you might want to try *roofingtalk.com*.

The important point is to break out of your shell and use the Internet to learn new tricks and techniques, make new contacts, and expand your horizons.

That will get you started. This section will also help you develop sales and marketing skills to increase your business. The subjects discussed are:

Marketing: the forgotten function
Hiring and training salespeople
Cold calling
Handling price objections

MARKETING: THE FORGOTTEN FUNCTION

The marketing function is the primary reason for success or failure of the trade contractor's enterprise, yet few contractors pay any attention to marketing. If they shift at least a portion of their focus to marketing without doubt they'll experience a boost in sales.

There are 21 key principles that you can analyze and use to develop a marketing plan, and two points to always remember: 1) The customer is always right and 2) Marketing is a skill that can be learned.

Principle Number One: Find a New Customer or Keep an Old Customer?

❖ It is always more expensive to create customers than to keep customers. So why do so many contractors continually try to find new customers and shun the focus on keeping the customers they already have? Possibly they don't know how to hold onto customers and find new customers at the same time, the purpose of marketing. *The purpose of marketing is to create perceptions of unique added value.* You retain customers by creating relationships with them and providing service and quality in all of your products and services.

Principle Number Two: There Are Four Main Approaches to Marketing Success.

❖ Create a product or service that satisfies a basic need.

❖ Pricing: Start low, gain market share, and use economies of scale to reduce price again.

❖ Adapt to a customer's reality. They expect high quality and will be satisfied with nothing less.

❖ Deliver true value *as perceived by your customers* (not as you see it. You must develop "customer eyes."). What represents value to your customer? There are two key words that answer this question: *niche* and *uniqueness.* Find a niche in the market where your uniqueness really makes a difference. For example, if you're installing skylights in   residential homes, perhaps you might find a ready market by installing solar panels, too.

Principle Number Three: Three Questions to Ask Regarding the Market.

❖ Is there a Market for your product or service? The 80/20 rule states that 80 percent of new products or services will fail, 20 percent of them will pay for themselves and of that 20 percent, 1 percent will be very successful. Bring out as many new products and services as economically feasible provided the market is receptive and the product or service profitable.
❖ Is the Market big enough? If it's too small or if it is crowded with competitors, your business may not survive.
❖ Is the Market concentrated enough? It can be spread out too far to deliver the product or service profitably. Delivery channels are often more important than the product or service.

Principle Number Four: All Successful Marketing Is Based on Good Research and Intelligence.

A focus group composed of your key customers is the best source to gather information. Key questions to ask:

❖ Who is your customer? Who buys it now, who bought it in the past, and what are their demographics?
❖ Where is your customer geographically? How will you deliver the product or service?
❖ How does your customer select and buy your contracting product and service?
❖ Why do they buy your product and service? What's the benefit for them and what do they need?
❖ Why do customers buy your product or service? What are customers going to do with it when they get it?

Principle Number Five: Customer Needs.

Need is a felt dissatisfaction, so your product or service has to satisfy that need. For example:

❖ Customers buy to be better off (improvement).
❖ Customers are interested in the benefit, not the product or service, but what they can enjoy (for example, a new home, or a new hot water heater).

❖ Buying the product or service will result in the feeling customers anticipate.

❖ Customers buy solutions to problems.

❖ Customers buy to save or earn time or money.

❖ Customers buy for gain or to avoid a loss.

❖ The more basic the need, the simpler or more direct the appeal; the more complex the need, the more subtle the appeal must be.

Principle Number Six: Competitive Analysis.

❖ Who or what is the competition? Examples: Who would be competitive trade contractors? What constitutes lack of knowledge about your product or service and how will it affect the customer's judgment of your offering?

❖ Why do people buy from your competition? What do they offer that you don't?

❖ Why should they switch to you? What advantages do you offer?

❖ What are your critical assumptions about the competition? Don't underestimate them.

❖ What are they doing right? Imitate them and do it better.

❖ What non-competitor can you join forces with to get a market advantage? As an example if you build porches you might be able to work with a retailer selling porch furniture to give the customer a package deal.

Principle Number Seven: Competitive Advantage (Perception of Unique Value = High Profits).

❖ Be the best at something and be sure that everyone in your business knows what that superior factor is. What is your advantage, what should it be, and what could it be? Make your product or service unique. *The purpose of marketing is to use your competitive advantage.*

Principle Number Eight: Who Will Be Your Competitors?

❖ What are their strengths and weaknesses?

❖ What will be their response to your intrusion into a market they now dominate? The purpose of moving into a new market is to gain share, not spend money defending your market position.

- ❖ What do you have to do differently than your competitor to grow, succeed and survive?
- ❖ Who will be your competitors tomorrow and what can you do to prepare for their entry into your market?

Principle Number Nine: Tactics of Diversion.
Diversion:

- ❖ Appear to be unworthy of attention; too small to bother with. That will catch your competition off-guard.
- ❖ Appear to be unbeatable; get market share quickly.
- ❖ Be secretive until you are ready to launch your business, a new product or new service.
- ❖ Redirect attention to low profit, high volume products or services.

Principle Number Ten: The Market Plan

- ❖ Product or service: Clearly state what it is and what it isn't.
- ❖ Price: Skim and Penetration
  Skim: Price it high and target innovators.
  Its weakness is that high profits draw competition.
  Penetration: Price it low to kill off competition.
  Its weakness is competition by pricing only is always a risky move.
- ❖ Place: Where is the product or service to be sold? For example, nation, region, state, store.
- ❖ Promotion: How are you going to advertise?
- ❖ Product, price, place, and promotion make up the marketing mix. Continually review the mix to increase market share and profits.

Principle Number Eleven: The First with the Most.

- ❖ Be the market leader. This approach is high risk and high profit.

Principle Number Twelve: Hit 'Em Where They Ain't.

- ❖ Introduce a new product or service into an existing market.
- ❖ Create an imitation, only do it better.

❖ Add something new or different to the product or service.

Principle Number Thirteen: Dominate a Niche.
- ❖ Tollgate: A product or service that everyone must have in order to enter an industry. For example, plumbing for a plumbing subcontractor and electrical skills for an electrical subcontractor, including state or county licensing.
- ❖ Specialty Skills: For example in a woodworking shop, the ability of your carpenters to make intricate scrollwork others will have difficulty imitating.
- ❖ Specialty Market: Perhaps your contracting company specializes in constructing bomb shelters while few if any other competitors can.

Principle Number Fourteen: Customer Focus.
- ❖ Successful marketing puts customers in the center and surrounds them with company communications, both going to customers and coming from them. Customer feedback drives the trade contracting business.

Principle Number Fifteen: Positioning.
- ❖ How do you want to be seen by your customers and what will they say about your business?
- ❖ How would it be useful to be perceived this way?
- ❖ What can you do to start that perception today?
- ❖ How can you position your product or service so it stands out from competition?

Principle Number Sixteen: Creative Marketing and Growth Strategy.

Markets

	Existing	New
List product or Service here		

In the diagram show above, list your products and services on the left and in the two boxes to the right describe the existing markets and what you want the new markets to be. This matrix will clarify your thinking.

- ❖ Sell more in an existing market. Combine products and services, develop or modify delivery systems, and reduce prices.
- ❖ Sell new products or services to existing customers.
- ❖ Find new markets for existing products or services.
- ❖ Sell new products or services in new markets using existing resources.
- ❖ "Bundle of Resources Concept": your company is a bundle of resources. What can it do besides what it is doing now with the same resources?

Principle Number Seventeen: What Other Ways Can You Sell Your Products or Services?

- ❖ There are multiple ways to sell, yet most trade contractors only use one or two. Here are some channels: online website, direct mail, telephone, retail, wholesale, manufacturers' representatives, distributors, multi-level marketing, franchise, newspapers, television, trade shows, and promotions.

Principle Number Eighteen: Look at New Products or Services You Can Create Using the Skills of Existing Employees.

- ❖ For example if you now build homes, why not use the same employees to build portable sheds that house lawn mowers and gardening equipment?
- ❖

Principle Number Nineteen: Distribution Channels.

Distribution Channels are often more important than the product or service; they remain after demand for the product or service declines.

- ❖ What additional products or services can you sell through an existing channel?
- ❖ What additional channels are there?
- ❖ What new products or services can you create for your existing channels?
- ❖ What new products or services can you create for new channels?

Principle Number Twenty: Market Research and Market Testing.
- Develop a bias for action; go to the customer and uncover problems and opportunities for your business.
- Ask customers. Develop a prototype, but do it fast (days, not months).
- The only real test is a market test. Will customers buy your products or services?
- Aim for immediate feedback.

Principle Number Twenty one: Four Keys to Marketing Success
- Specialization: Only go into markets where you can offer better value.
- Differentiation: The key to profits. How can you differentiate your product or service from competitors?
- Segmentation: Look for a market segment that you have the resources and skills to handle, particularly from customers who are willing to pay a premium price.
- Concentration: Focus on the market segment where you can sell the most of your products or services at the highest price.

HIRING AND TRAINING SALESPEOPLE

If you can't sell your products and services you're going out of business in a hurry. If you can't sell your products and services at a price that is profitable, you're still going out of business. That's where a talented sales force comes in. Their mission is to sell your trade contractor offering and sell it at a profit. And that takes a special set of skills. You need to hire and train salespeople who can deliver the goods. This procedure explains how.

1.0 Products and Services That Satisfy Customers

1.0   The purpose of this procedure is to establish and describe the sales policies and procedures for ABC Contractors., Inc. It is the function of sales to sell products and services that best satisfy the needs of customers and return the highest profits for the trace contractor.

2.0 Desired Salesperson Characteristics

2.1   A salesperson should possess honorable traits of character, including a high degree of honesty, responsibility, loyalty, progressiveness, sincerity, good mannerisms, and positive attitudes, tempered with thought. The former days of bluff and hearty salespeople (mostly men) with their phony, insincere approach to customers is long gone. And thankfully so. Customers today are better educated and suspicious of salespeople who sell the sizzle but not the steak. They are more tuned in to quality and value and insist upon it in their products and services.

2.2   Experience in sales is important. A professional look and neat appearance are essential. The desire to succeed and a willingness to support the contractor's programs and policies are absolutely necessary.

3.0 Responsibilities

3.1   Representing himself, the company, and all of its products and services loyally and faithfully, and in accordance with policy and instruction.

3.2   Gaining a thorough knowledge of the contractor's services and their applications. Remaining current with technological advances and changes in the industry.

3.3   Completion and maintenance of records, reports, customer profiles, call reports, order forms, and other customer data, as required.

3.4   Maintaining an attitude of confidence in the company, its products, suppliers, and customers.

3.5   Carrying the required liability insurance on any personal automobile used for business purposes. Proof of insurance must be furnished to the company and on file in the salesperson's personnel file.

4.0 Performance

4.1   Sell enough volume of sales to meet the realistic attainable projection for the salesperson's territory or assigned accounts.

4.2   Contact and maintain relationships with all customers and potential customers. Prospect and develop new customers.

4.3   Commit to an honest day's work. Eight hours is not always sufficient to achieve the company's sales goals. Sales orders are proportional to the number of calls and quotes, and that often means extra hours.

4.4   Follow all procedures for reporting sales, lost sales, call reports, itineraries, quotations, expense reports, and other necessary documentation on time.

4.5   Maintain sales manuals and documents in current and good order.

4.6   Build and maintain a high degree of confidence and acceptance with customers and fellow employees.

4.7   Follow every sale from beginning through completion to see that all details are handled accurately and effectively. No sale is complete until the product or service is delivered, installed, invoiced, and collected. The result must be a satisfied customer.

4.8   Continue prospecting and generating new sales opportunities.

4.9   Share leads and useful or pertinent information with other salespeople for the company's benefit. Be a team player.

5.0 Limitations

5.1   Salespeople do not have the authority to obligate the company on any contract, agreement, or sale unless specific authorization has been granted by the company owner or manager. Sales orders are subject to approval and acceptance by the company.

5.2   Sales manuals and all literature are the property of the company, and are to be handled in a safe, confidential manner.

5.3   Improper attention and coverage of accounts is cause for removal of those accounts from a salesperson's responsibility. An account that has not been contacted for three months is not receiving proper attention (high sales level accounts should be contacted weekly, if not daily). Any longtime account with no sales for six months may be considered to be receiving ineffective coverage.

5.4   Failure to maintain his quota for a three-month period is reason for review and possible dismissal.

5.5   A salesperson does not have direct supervisory capacity over other company employees. He should be aware of the chain of command and respect the authority of designated supervisors in a cooperative manner.

5.6   Full time salespeople must not engage in any other gainful employment or perform services for any other company for compensation of any type without the full knowledge and approval by the company owner.

5.7   The company reserves the right to deem customers as house accounts. A house account requires no commission and is to be considered the responsibility of the company owner or manager.

6.0 Company Support

6.1   New salespeople will receive training from management and existing sales staff.

6.2   Territories are assigned and protected. No infringement will be made without advance discussion, or agreement in accordance with company procedures.

6.3   The company will endeavor to maintain high standards of sales support with inventory, service, sales aids, sales leads, advertising, business cards, and sales and technical literature.

COLD CALLING

More often than not, the business of a trade contractor rests on the ability of one or more of its employees to cold call potential customers. This is how most small companies launch, and in its early years particularly, the success or failure of the business is tied to its effectiveness at turning cold call recipients into hot prospects. Once telemarketers set appointments the company's salesperson takes over and hopefully converts hot prospects into paying customers.

Cold calling from lists of names is a numbers game: the more calls your telemarketer makes, the more sales appointments he secures. The more sales appointments he secures, the more (face-to-face) sales calls the company salesperson makes. The more sales calls the salesperson makes, the more customers the trade contractor gets. It's as simple as that. But it takes a lot of hard work and perseverance.

For most businesses, the expectation is that of every 100 phone calls made by a telemarketer, he will set about two face-to-face sales calls for the salesperson. The salesperson can expect to convert a sales call to an actual order about one in ten times (although that number will vary, depending on the cost of the services provided by the contractor. Here's the cold call to sales pyramid:

Cold calls made	500
Sales calls made	10
Sales orders taken	1

Obviously these numbers will vary, depending on products and services offered by the trade contractor. It takes a lot of time and effort and schmoozing of customers, for example, for the trade contractor to win a contract for paving twenty miles of county roads, while the trade contractor removing dead trees and mowing lawns for residential properties sells his services quickly.

But, on average, it takes 500 phone calls to produce one actual order. A tough business, indeed, but one that most contractors face at one time or another during the course of running their businesses.

The following procedure describes how to run an effective cold calling operation.

1.0 Launching the Program

1.1 The purpose of this procedure is to establish the outline for a training program at the contractor's company, given to selected employees concerning how to telemarket non-introductory (cold) sales calls.

2.0 Cold Calling

2.1 So-called cold calling is the best and most economical method to develop new customers you don't currently have.

2.2 Making cold calls is difficult for practically everyone because the concept triggers a basic human emotion, the fear of rejection. Imagine making 1000 phone calls and being turned down 996 times. It takes a special type of person to weather that extent of negative responses day in, day out and come back the next day.

2.3 Many companies have developed a two-phase format for cold calling, which they have found effective:

❖ First is a telephoned cold call. This is a type of limited telemarketing, the purpose being to arrange an onsite sales call rather than taking an order for a product or service.

❖ Studies made at the Wharton School of Business, indicate that employees are often more comfortable making initial approaches on the telephone instead of face to face.

❖ For some as yet scientifically unexplainable reason, many executives will occasionally interrupt an important meeting to take a stranger's telephone call. Those same executives will refuse to see unscheduled visitors who have taken the time and effort to travel across the country to see them.

3.0 The Follow-Up Sales Call

3.1 Telemarketing is followed by the salesperson who is now a scheduled (therefore anointed) visitor.

3.2 It has been determined that this two-phased cold call method works best when the telemarketer and the salesperson are different people. But it will work with one person taking both roles. Unfortunately, the types of people who sell face to face are frequently ineffective at selling sales appointment by phone. They are not the same skills.

4.0 Rules for Cold Calling

4.1 Cold calling has the best chance of success if you follow these rules:

❖ Be proud of your appearance. It's been proven that if you feel unkempt you will project that image over the telephone.

❖ While telemarketing, talk to your image in a mirror on your desk. Smile. It will come through in your voice.

❖ Say your piece, then listen and take notes. It is impossible to overcome objections if you don't hear them. Sometimes prospects do not say they object to something in the telemarketing spiel but they do nevertheless. The astute telemarketer will be able to "hear" an objection without it being stated.

❖ Be polite, be enthusiastic. Your voice is all you have going for you.

❖ Remember, you are not selling the company's products and services, but simply arranging to set sales appointments.

❖ Many telemarketers give up too readily in their attempts at setting appointments. As I mentioned earlier, it takes a special type of person to handle that kind of rejection.

5.0 Seven Steps to Help Make Cold Calling Easier

5.1 Get the prospect's attention. Do not just say hello and start your spiel. Instead tell the person at the end of the line (your potential customer) it is a call to borrow some of their time. If he is too busy to talk now, ask if you may call him back. Suggest a time. "May I call back between three and five this afternoon?"

5.2 Have an outlined script. It need not be formal or complete, but you need to keep on track. *Do not memorize it.* The prospect will be able to tell the difference, and may feel insulted.

5.3 Identify yourself by name and organization.

5.4 Specify the exact reason for the call.

5.5 If you get a yes, set an exact day and time for the appointment.

5.6 If the prospect has a strong negative response to your call, do not press the matter. Thank the person at the other end of the line and hang up.

5.7 No matter how else the call has gone, be polite and thank the prospect for his time and patience.

6.0 Cold Call Details

6.1   Once you've set the appointment, thank the prospect, and hang up, temporarily stop any further calls and:

- ❖ Fill out a prospect sheet for the salesperson.
- ❖ Detail the business called, the prospect's name, the time of appointment, and the telephone number with extension by which you made contact.

6.2   As the salesperson with a telemarketing appointment, you are still making a cold call. Do not forget this. The prospect has yet to be sold. Your job is to make the sale.

6.3   Do not assume an appointment means the contact really wants to see you; the telephone call may have caught him at a weak moment.

6.5   Know as much as possible about your potential customer. How big the account, how many locations, who is your competition, whom are you talking to and what is his position in the company. Amazingly enough, many of these answers will come from his secretary, if you know how to ask. Of course, if your customer is a homeowner or homemaker, you will not encounter a secretary or administrative assistant, but the need for you to know enough about the prospect's needs remains the same.

6.6   What you do not know by the time you sit with the prospect, ask. Do not be afraid to verify what you think you know. People generally like to dispense knowledge.

6.7   Do not attempt to overwhelm the prospect with your technical knowledge. Present your company's product and service capabilities and hand out any brochures you have that establish the credibility of your company. If the prospect wants to know more, he will ask.

6.8   Remember that the sales call is successful *only* if you get an order for your company's products and services.

HANDLING PRICE OBJECTIONS

1.0   The Erosion of Profits

This standard procedure describes one of the methods of overcoming the most common objection in a sale: price. Regardless of whether you're dealing with businesspeople or consumers you have to be able to counter reasons for lowering the price of your products and services. Guaranteed! Not all prospects, of course, but most of them. Everybody loves to haggle over price. And every time you lower your company's price for its offered goods and services you are, in effect, lowering your company's profits. That's the kind of erosion that eats away at your company's vitality. In the short run, it's an easy way to sell; in the long run it damages both you and your company.

2.0   Overcoming Price Objections

If you have been a professional salesperson for number of years you experienced the subject of price objections arising in virtually every sales meeting you attended. So, knowing that price objections are coming, why not prepare for it and deliver an eloquent response, and in the process put some extra bread in your pocket? (Since price cuts also cut into your commission.)

This is not to say that a prepared response will overcome the objection every time; rather a prepared response will increase your chances of success.

The Challenge

Imagine that you are an installer of large foyer and bathroom tiles, selling at $1 each. You have a competitor who reduced his price to $.90. While the 10 cent price differential may not seem significant to you, the prospect, a builder of palatial-sized homes operating on thin margins, is about to place a large order. If you take the ten cent differential and multiply it by the number of tiles the prospect is going to purchase, the prospect will spend $100,000 more with your company. *That's an automatic red flag.* Keep in mind that times are tough and the prospect is having trouble justifying the more expensive purchase from you. The challenge is to justify the price differential. What do you do?

Quality

Typically, many salespeople will respond by saying that their products have the
best quality. They try to use the issue of quality without taking the time to quantify the bottom line impact for their prospects. A big mistake.

If this sounds familiar, it should. Most salespeople sell this way. They think quality is a one-word cure for any and all price objections.

Take a moment to think about your competitors. If you're touting the quality of your products and services, what do you think they're doing? Be assured they're also touting the exact same thing. Unfortunately, if you are talking about product and service quality and your competition is talking the same game, you have done little to differentiate yourself. You are still left with the $100,000 price differential.

Value

Instead, raise the issue of value. The only way to respond to the price differential challenge is to raise the visibility of the value of the offer contained in your proposal. *Customers will always buy on price until you show them that the price of a product or service is only one element of the total cost of ownership.* But it's up to you to show them. They may not realize how much of a difference it means.

All other things being equal, the customer may be looking for the lowest price; however, in sales, all other sales advantages are seldom equal. Customers use price as a decision-making point because it is the easiest way to compare two completely different offerings. *If you are able to differentiate your offering on price alone, then let your customers know what they really want is not the lowest price but the lowest total-cost solution.* The lowest total-cost model of selling tells the customer that every buying decision has implications.

In another example, if Mr. Prospect buys sub-standard electrical wiring, he may have a fire on hands. Your job as sales professionals is to raise the visibility of these implications. *The best way to raise the visibility of value is to quantify the impact of your recommendations.* Show the customer that your ideas have a tangible bottom-line impact on his business.

The comparison shown at the end of this chapter describes how to quantify the impact of the value of your product, using the case of the large tile sale. Here you assumed that you could reduce the customer's cost in three specific areas, and you have assigned dollar value to those areas. If you were to compare the two suppliers (you and your competitor) on the basis of invoice cost for the tiles alone, most prospects would choose your competitor. The focal point of that decision would obviously be price.

However, *while price is clearly one element of a sales transaction, there are other elements that need to be considered.* Your job is to raise the visibility of these other elements. As you can see from the example shown at the end of this chapter, once you factor these other elements into the equation, *you are really offering the customer the lowest total-cost solution.* In our example, you are saving the customer $10,000 over the option presented by the competition.

Conclusion

In order to be successful at value selling, you must become adept at raising the visibility of *all* the value elements of the sales transaction. Whenever the issue of price arises, remember this field-tested process:

❖ Prepare for price objection.
❖ Raise the visibility of the value issue.
❖ Quantify the impact of your value proposal.

HANDLING PRICE OBJECTION EXAMPLE

	Your Company	The Competition
Invoiced Cost	$100,000	$90,000
Shipping efficiency	($5,000)	0
Installation efficiencies	($15,000)	0
True Cost	$80,000	$90,000

Of course, to make this option work your technical people must devise methods for obtaining shipping and installation efficiencies. But, after all, that is playing to your strong suit: you are a master at the technical side of your business.

A note to my readers:

Congratulations on digesting the six major parts of this book. You have made an investment and a commitment to strengthen your business and insulate it from failure. Change is not difficult once you recognize what needs to be changed, how your employees will help you achieve it, and you have a plan that you can execute *now.* Seize the moment and remember that *nothing changes if nothing changes*. Good luck and enjoy the process.

Jim McCain

END

APPENDIX

The following pages contain:

A one-page description of Jim McCain and his services

Examples of types of trade contractors and subcontractors

ONE PAGE SUMMARY OF BOOK AND AUTHOR

Dr. James (Jim) McCain, The Business Doctor ◆ Business Works ◆ http://www.bizdrsolution.com/ 541 Waite Road ◆ Rexford, NY 12148
◆ 518-383-3337 ◆ *jim@bizdrsolution.com*

Jim McCain
Ph.D.
The
Business Doctor

Founder and
Owner of
Business Works

HOW *BUSINESS*
WORKS CAN HELP
THE TRADES
CONTRACTOR

Business systems

Business Products

Consulting Services

Business Documents

Business Procedures

WHY TRADE CONTRACTORS FAIL AND HOW TO PREVENT IT

Thirty Years Helping Small Businesses Survive and Prosper

A Book by
Jim McCain

Jim McCain, *The Business Doctor*, founder and CEO of Business Works, packs his book with tips and techniques that will resolve your business problems and get your trades contracting company up and running in record time with record results.

He has earned his title *The Business Doctor*. During his career Jim consulted with almost 450 companies such as yours, many of them trades contractors . . . and has solved complex and intractable problems that otherwise would have bankrupted their businesses.

Jim's clients know he can get the job done:

"The most important aspects of your consulting work were in the areas of measuring performance, with a revised review process which will address the accountability issues. Effective budgets and their use will be a big improvement. We are satisfied that the recommendations and actions will allow us to tackle the main issues." KB, President Plumbing, Heating and Air Conditioning Supply Company Selkirk, NY

"I am writing at the conclusion of the work completed by Jim McCain. I feel that the analysis of my company was thorough and complete in developing an accurate financial picture of my company. The services I received will allow me to better understand the true costs of running my business. We are satisfied with the work completed." SPB Landscaping, Design and Maintenance Company Cohasset, MA

Examples of Types of Trade Contractors and Subcontractors (as reported by USA Contractors Search online:iii)

This section describes types of trade contractors and subcontractors. The list is fairly inclusive and is meant only as an indication of the types of specialties involved.

Trade Contractors

General Contractor

Building Contractor

Residential Contractor

Air Conditioning/ Heat Contractor

Electrical Contractor

Internal Pollutant Storage Tank Lining Applicators

Precision Tank Testers

Plumbing Contractors

Pool/ Spa Contractors

Roofing Contractors

Sheet Metal Contractors

Solar Contractors

Underground Utility & Excavation Contractors

Specialty Contractors

1. Gas Line

2. Glass & Glazing

3. Gypsum Drywall

4. Marine

5. Pollutant Storage Systems

6. Residential Solar Water Heating

7. Structure

Trade Subcontractors

AC Duct Cleaners

Aluminum Contractors

Asbestos Removal/ Service

Awning Installers

Block Masons

Brick Masons

Cabinet Makers

Cabinet Installers

Carpet Installers

Cleaning Services

Closet Shelving

Commercial Door Installers

Commercial Window Installers

Concrete Footings & Foundations

Concrete Finishers

Concrete Pumping Services

Countertop Installers

Crane Services

Custom Wood Cutters

Deck Construction

Demolition Services

Docks/ Boathouse Construction

Drafting & Design

Drywall Stockers

Drywall Hangers

Drywall Finishers

Elevator Contractors/ Service

Fence Installers

Fireplace & Wood Stove Installers

Fireproofing

Fountain & Pond Installers

Framers

Garage Door Installers

Glass & Mirror Cutting/ Installers

Gutter Installers

Handyman Services

Home Entertainment Systems

Home Inspection Services

Home Maintenance Services

Hurricane Shutter Installers

HVAC Designs and Load Calculations

Insulation Installers

Interior Design & Decorators

Irrigation Installers/ Service

Land Clearing

Landscaping

Lawn Maintenance

Lightning Rod Installers

Line Locators

Logging Services

Metal Framers

Mold & Mildew Services

Moving Services

Outdoor Playground Builders

Painters

Paving

Permit Services

Pest Control Services

Powder Coating

Residential Door Installers

Residential Window Installers

Sandblasting Services

Seal Coating Services

Security Systems

Septic Tank Pumping

Signage and Lettering

Sinkhole Repair

Site Clearing

Skylight Installers

Snow Removal Services

Soffit/ Siding Installers

Stained Glass

Stairs/ Railing

Stone Masons

Striping and Marking Services

Structural Moving & Rigging

Stucco Finishers

Stump Grinding

Thermal Imaging

Tile Installers/ Repair

Tree Trimming

Trim Carpenters

Wall Coverings Wallpaper

Waste Material Removal

Water Treatment Systems

Waterproofing

Welders

Well Drilling

Window Coverings/ Tinting

Wood Flooring Installers/ Finishers

---

[i] http://ecmweb.com/mag/electric_contractor_failure_rate/
[ii] To simplify matters I will be using the word "he" in this book to refer to either sex.
[iii] http://uscontractorssearch.com/about_us.html

www.ingramcontent.com/pod-product-compliance
Lightning Source LLC
Chambersburg PA
CBHW031810190326
41518CB00006B/270